The L!BRARY Book

The

L!BR

Book
Design Collaborations in the Public Schools
Anooradha Iyer Siddiqi

Princeton Architectural Press
New York

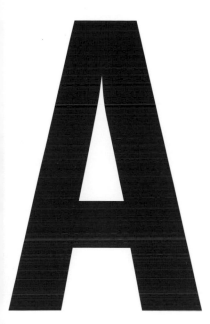

For New York City,
whose subways are mobile reading rooms

Published by
Princeton Architectural Press
37 East Seventh Street
New York, New York 10003

For a free catalog of books,
call 1.800.722.6657.
Visit our website at www.papress.com.

Editor: Jennifer Thompson
Designer: Pentagram

Special thanks to: Nettie Aljian, Bree Anne Apperley,
Sara Bader, Nicola Bednarek, Janet Behning,
Becca Casbon, Carina Cha, Penny (Yuen Pik) Chu,
Carolyn Deuschle, Russell Fernandez, Pete Fitzpatrick,
Wendy Fuller, Jan Haux, Clare Jacobson, Aileen Kwun,
Nancy Eklund Later, Linda Lee, Laurie Manfra,
John Myers, Katharine Myers, Dan Simon,
Andrew Stepanian, Paul Wagner, Joseph Weston, and
Deb Wood of Princeton Architectural Press
—Kevin C. Lippert, publisher

ROBIN HOOD

PUBLIC ARCHITECTURE
PUTS THE RESOURCES OF ARCHITECTURE IN THE SERVICE OF THE
PUBLIC INTEREST. WE IDENTIFY AND SOLVE PRACTICAL PROBLEMS
OF HUMAN INTERACTION IN THE BUILT ENVIRONMENT AND ACT
AS A CATALYST FOR PUBLIC DISCOURSE THROUGH EDUCATION,
ADVOCACY AND THE DESIGN OF PUBLIC SPACES AND AMENITIES.
1211 FOLSOM STREET, 4TH FLOOR, SAN FRANCISCO, CA 94103-3816
T 415.861.8200 F 415.431.9695 WWW.PUBLICARCHITECTURE.ORG

NATIONAL
ENDOWMENT
FOR THE ARTS

Library of Congress Cataloging-in-Publication Data

Siddiqi, Anooradha Iyer.
 The l!brary book : design collaborations in the public
schools / Anooradha Iyer Siddiqi.
    p. cm.
 ISBN 978-1-56898-832-0 (alk. paper)
1. Library buildings--New York (State)--New York--
Design and construction. 2. School libraries--New York
(State)--New York--Planning. 3. Library architecture--
New York (State)--New York. 4. Public schools--New York
(State)--New York--Case studies. 5. L!brary Initiative
(New York, N.Y.) I. Title. II. Title: Library book.
 Z679.2.U54I94 2009
 727'.828097471--dc22
                                        2009014528

Contents

Preface

During my brief tenure as director of the L!brary Initiative at Robin Hood, two critical issues caught my attention. First, a concern for making new kinds of libraries for children seemed to be brewing in many corners of the world. Second, despite its celebration of books, this initiative had no book about itself. Having known about the L!brary Initiative first as a fan, then as a journalist, and finally as one of the many collaborators who worked to see it through, I have hoped for a publication that would cast its ideas beyond New York, but also record it for many of the participants in the schools, whose busy days keep them from traveling to other libraries to see the lattice they are creating to support children.

The network of libraries suggests a cultural idea bigger than any one school's work. Also, while the particulars of this initiative may be unique to New York, the idea is replicable beyond this city. I hope that this publication amplifies the good spirit of the L!brary Initiative by extending its own shelf life and sketching a case study for similar endeavors elsewhere. Based on interviews with diverse participants and contributions from all the designers, this document is meant to capture some of the L!brary Initiative's visual artifacts and transmit key ideas behind an innovative interpretation of a classic institution.

The art and architecture in these pages is only a fragment of the scope and agenda of this Initiative. Nonetheless, design of this caliber rarely serves clients whose need is not matched by means. The beauty in these images—as echoed by many, from cash donors to school principals—lies not in their aesthetics but in the action they represent.

Anooradha Iyer Siddiqi
New York City

Notes on the Text

The L!brary Initiative is a vast collaboration. The breadth of this project and a need to condense its text has often limited the acknowledgement of individuals to the institutions, organizations, or firms they associated with. Other forms of collective acknowledgement are explained below. These are meant to simplify the text, albeit at the risk of suppressing deeper complexities.

"L!brary Initiative" herein refers to a joint private-public venture in New York City that began in 2000. The program's private partner, the Robin Hood Foundation (a.k.a. Robin Hood), led by Executive Director David Saltzman, is a not-for-profit granting organization that has targeted poverty in the five boroughs since 1988 by applying strategic investment principles to philanthropy. The organization does not run programs, but finds, funds, assists, and evaluates organizations that fight poverty in the arenas of early childhood and youth, education, jobs and economic security, survival, and emergency relief— making annual grants in the hundred-million dollar range in recent years. Under the L!brary Initiative, Robin Hood has independently funded libraries in several charter schools, including one at Beginning with Children Charter School in Brooklyn that served as a prototype for those in these pages. However, this book will focus on projects executed jointly with the New York City Department of Education.

The L!brary Initiative was founded under a board of education led by former Chancellor Harold Levy that operated independently of the New York City government. In 2002, the New York State Legislature granted Mayor Michael Bloomberg control over the New York City public school system and the Initiative continued under Chancellor Joel Klein's leadership. The Fund for Public Schools, a not-for-profit organization whose mission is in part to attract private investment in the public schools, develops partnerships between the Department of Education and private investors like Robin Hood. The organization has actively liaised between the two in recent years to implement the L!brary Initiative. The School Construction Authority has been an independent agency for the duration of the L!brary Initiative, and is currently one of its partners in implementing the design and construction of libraries. "Department of Education" herein denotes the Board and/or the Department. Because of the close connections these parties and the Mayor's office have had with the L!brary Initiative, the "City of New York" or the "City" often refer to the parties that are directly responsible for or representative of the New York City public schools— those on the "public" side of the partnership, including the private Fund that offers support to the system.

School designations and data reflect what they were at the time schools were selected for participation, though some of the elementary schools have expanded to add middle schools. Nomenclature for the New York City public schools includes abbreviation by school type and separate numbering by borough, with the following designations:

P.S. = Public School
C.S. = Community School
M.S. = Middle School

X=Bronx
K=Brooklyn
M=Manhattan
Q=Queens
R=Staten Island

For instance,

P.S. 18R = Public School 18 in Staten Island
C.S. 50X = Community School 50 in the Bronx
M.S. 88K = Middle School 88 in Brooklyn.

School grades are designated as follows:

Pre-K = Pre-kindergarten (children aged four years by December 31)
K-5 = elementary school
K-8 = elementary and middle school

Portions of this text were previously published in "Case Studies on Collaboration: Lessons Learned from the Library Initiative," in *AIA Report on University Research* (Volume 2, 2006), and "The Art of the Library," in *Jamini: An International Arts Quarterly* (Volume 4, Number 2, "The New Architecture," January 2008).

Those responsible for the visual expression of the libraries are often listed collectively rather than under the conventional demarcations of the design professions, matching the spirit in which the individual imprints of participants from other disciplines—education, government, business, and so on—are collectively acknowledged.

New Libraries for New York

What would happen if you cast reading as a pivotal life experience? The story of the L!brary Initiative is the story of that gamble. The projects in these pages—the literal and figurative exclamation points at the heart of this story—bet on the power of a transformational environment.

In 2001, the library doors opened at Community School 50 in the Bronx, the first project in an ambitious initiative under the New York City Board of Education and the Robin Hood Foundation. The City and the not-for-profit organization experimented with the makeover of an institution that captured the imagination of many who partnered to foster its reincarnation. They targeted the library in the largest public school system in the United States, aiming to undercut poverty by making rousing places for learning in some of the poorest neighborhoods of New York.

Rather than tackle educational reform incrementally, the partners sought to revolutionize the library as a driver in the academic and cultural life of the school. Strategically, this meant reimagining what a school library and its components might be, and tactically, this meant embedding the library in the classroom and the larger institution. The new resource would have an uncommon architectural expression. The highest-quality materials and technology would equip it. The library would be open after school and in the summers so parents could visit and read with their children. The best teachers would become the librarians. They would be university-trained to make innovative use of the library resources. They would become leaders in the school. Librarians and classroom teachers together would creatively promote students' sense of inquiry. Principals would actively integrate the library into the agenda and the daily life of the school. A range of partners would breathe new life into the resource: corporate and individual underwriters, children's book publishers, architects and designers, construction teams, product and technology manufacturers, universities, library associations, educators, bureaucrats, the press, and of course, the administrators, teachers, and students in the fray.

Their experiments follow.

Inaugurating the L!brary Initiative, interior designer Karen Davidov waited for the final furniture delivery at the site of C.S. 50X, viewing lower Manhattan out these windows on the morning of September 11, 2001. The graphic perimeter frieze of students' poems had been designed to mimic the New York City skyline.

L!brary Initiative schools either lacked a library or had a stagnating collection. Many outdated titles like this stopped circulating in the 1960s. Early Initiative partners like Scholastic helped to establish literary currency by pledging one million books to the base collections of 7,500 books provided to each school by Robin Hood.

A high school graduate earns over $10,000 more annually and is healthier than a high school dropout.[3] Encouraging an early love of reading and a desire to learn is a strategy to keep students in school.

L!brary Initiative Strategy (from the mission statement):

Redefine the mission of the library as a resource for the entire school community.

Rebuild the library with new design standards and unique imagery.

Replenish the library with new books and technology.

Retrain school staff to make full use of the library.

Reassess the impact of the school library to track progress and impact.

The Power of a Good Idea

"A book is like having a teacher right in your hands."[1]

The L!brary Initiative was conceived under the creative vision and organizational efforts of Lonni Tanner at Robin Hood and Jonathan Levi at the Board of Education. They targeted literacy in a school system serving 1.1 million children, where more than half of elementary students were reading below standard for their grade level. The project aligned with Robin Hood's mission to attack poverty at its roots—in this case, through education. Robin Hood initiated a series of discussions among a group of educators and designers who were invited to consider wholly new spaces and modes for intellectual and social discourse in public elementary schools, some serving over a thousand students in one building. This group considered instructional practice and facilities in combination, imagining a loud, creative place where multiple class groups and lone individuals would simultaneously engage in diverse activities. In schools that often did not have a library, or where books were outdated or had not been checked out for decades, the library was meant to become a new locus for culture.[2]

Nearly ten percent of the City's public schools have participated in the L!brary Initiative, rendering over fifty libraries as platforms for innovative instruction and a uniformly high caliber of architectural design. The L!brary Initiative has built, stocked, equipped, and maintained libraries, from a pilot group in ten schools identified in 2000 to the most recent opened in 2008. Its funding and operations structure has drawn jointly from resources in the public and private sectors. Robin Hood entered into collaborative partnership with the public schools following its own experiments to innovate educational approaches, and the partnership has survived restructuring through multiple City administrations. As products of an initiative that directly involved luminaries in public service, philanthropy, education, and design, the libraries attest to the willingness of individuals at many levels to put their heads down and find solutions. Perhaps the power of a good idea prevailed.

The Initiative has encouraged cooperative instruction, requiring that teachers and librarians jointly enhance and deliver curriculum, actuating the library as an agent in the educational process instead of a mere placeholder.[4] It has required teachers to become credentialed librarians, covering tuition for them to attend a graduate program in Library Science created especially for them at Syracuse University. It has sought to integrate a host of academic resources, including a diverse base collection of current literature, state-of-the-art computer technology, salaried staff with appropriate training, programs during and after school that educate students, parents, and teachers, and public access outside of school hours and in the summers to engage the greater community.

The Initiative's results have been complex, robust, and multidisciplinary. The following pages explore how design and notions of place have shaped the problem to be solved, both in terms of what has been built and in the processes for reconsidering the institutions of school and library. Alongside its efforts in education and philanthropy, the L!brary Initiative has been an essay in both the conceptual and social aspirations of art and architecture. As such, it might be useful to consider its myriad aspects as illuminated by certain precedents.

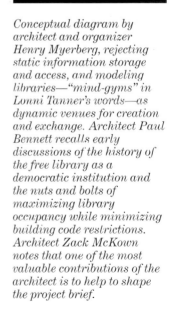

Before and after, at P.S. 93X

Good Environment

The L!brary Initiative has produced a dynamic design exercise amounting to a call to action, and granted architects an unusual measure of freedom in exploration. Architects offered more than just project implementation; many worked at the level of the overview to conceptualize the Initiative, determining new library functions, the architectural program, and a scalable project that could produce multiple roll-outs. They also managed the design process of individual projects, including mobilizing the donation of in-kind products and engineering services, and directing teams of artists and fabricators in the research and development of design for children. Robin Hood selected the participating architects based on reputation and professional record.

Rarely in modern history has a single private sponsor commissioned multiple investigations of one type of architecture. Consider *Arts & Architecture* editor John Entenza asking a handful of architects to develop prototypes for the modern home in 1945:

> The goal of the program was simply "good environment," and to achieve this the eight architects asked to participate were invited to experiment in form or materials…there were no restrictions on what they designed.[5]

The eight pilot projects of the legendary Case Study House Program led to thirty-six prototypes for residential design. Entenza's announcement "to take a plot of God's green earth and create 'good' living conditions" demanded artistic currency, offering in return a flexible model of patronage circumscribed within the parameters that the projects be "designed within a specified budget, subject, of course, to the dictates of price fluctuation" and "to the usual (and sometimes regrettable) building restrictions."[6]

Conceptual diagram by architect and organizer Henry Myerberg, rejecting static information storage and access, and modeling libraries—"mind-gyms" in Lonni Tanner's words—as dynamic venues for creation and exchange. Architect Paul Bennett recalls early discussions of the history of the free library as a democratic institution and the nuts and bolts of maximizing library occupancy while minimizing building code restrictions. Architect Zack McKown notes that one of the most valuable contributions of the architect is to help to shape the project brief.

ABOVE AND BELOW:
Mushroom-cap stools pepper
the pilot projects.

Architecture firms involved
with the pilot included Tod
Williams Billie Tsien
Architects (P.S. 101M, above),
Ronnette Riley Architect
(P.S. 149M, below), Deborah
Berke & Partners Architects
(P.S. 46M), Della Valle
Bernheimer (P.S. 18R), Tsao
& McKown (P.S. 19Q), Weiss/
Manfredi Architecture/
Landscape/Urbanism (P.S.
42Q), Helfand Myerberg
Guggenheimer Architects
(C.S. 50X), Gorlin Architects
(P.S. 92X), Richard H. Lewis
Architect (P.S. 165K), and
Paul Bennett Architect (P.S.
184K). Tucker Viemeister
brought his design expertise
to the creation of an identity
around the L!brary
Initiative.

Robin Hood has similarly approached architectural patronage with pragmatic generosity. Many L!brary Initiative architects distinguish the organization for its inclination and ability to support design experimentation within the rubric of redressing poverty. In practice, this has meant that Robin Hood commissions custom designs in institutional buildings; in terms of policy, the organization has been credited with instituting interdisciplinary planning forums to consider the restructuring of the public school library. The ten architects invited to develop the pilot each investigated a separate school site, reviewing them on several occasions with a group that included selected educators and library science professionals to find the most thought-provoking function and visual expression for a school library. Together they developed a theoretical framework for the new library, considering educational reform, literacy in language and design, and cultural values. Their cooperative practice yielded model guidelines for design. Participating firms have continued to share information informally but retained individual approaches to each project, so a piece of furniture might have appeared in multiple projects, even if a cabinet detail did not.

As with the Case Study houses, this theoretical process of investigation was predicated upon construction concerns. Designers addressed all the issues, both imaginative and mundane, that might be encountered in a room of 1,700 square feet. Restrictions on design generally followed issues of safety and security associated with construction upon school premises, moderation of cost, integration of modern infrastructural systems into decades-old buildings, and adherence to an administrative bureaucracy exceeding the usual for projects of this scope. Breakthroughs in design, conversely, have sprung from creative approaches to architectural programming, materials, and detailing, and the real-world testing of environments intended to engage students in a spirited learning process.

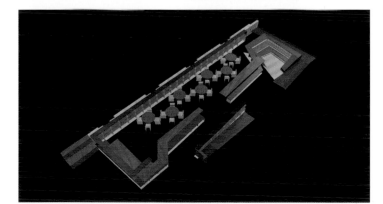

ABOVE: The element that unifies all the libraries is the bookshelf. Nearly every L!brary architect has cited millwork fabrication and procurement as the critical area where project cost and quality might be better controlled with repetition of details, although the expression of the unique hand of each architect has captivated schools and project sponsors alike.

MIDDLE RIGHT: Supporting the architect's concept of a contoured terrain, Pentagram telegraphed the L!brary logo's exclamation points onto the window glass— raindrops between earth and sky.

BOTTOM/MIDDLE LEFT: P.S. 151Q librarian Lorraine McKenna and Dean/Wolf Architects created one of the Initiative's most sumptuous libraries, using custom hardwood millwork to interrogate how a landscape for children might look and feel.

Major Carnegie library
design elements:

Prominent entrance

Large librarian desk at entry
for control and book
circulation

Large reading tables and
stacks for browsing

Natural light

Recognizable layout and high
quality architectural
detailing

If the librarian's job is to provoke children's intellectual engagement, then perhaps the architect's job is to evoke their sensibilities. The libraries serve children with likely no other exposure to "high" art or architecture, some with adverse learning difficulties, and many for whom the school is a refuge from a grim home or neighborhood. As such, most of the architects have proffered designs that are intellectually, emotionally, and sensorially accessible to the uninitiated—living rooms for the community at large.[7] Designers often textured the spaces with plush rugs and cozy sofas to associate reading with comfort and to invite adults to read with children, leveraging parents as a child's greatest resource.

Nearly all the libraries sought to manifest concepts of enlightenment and edification, not unlike the Carnegie libraries attempted a century earlier. Many sited the libraries prominently in relation to their physical surroundings, flooding reading rooms with natural daylight and housing books in open stacks to encourage browsing. In another nod to the Carnegie forbears, the circulation desk—manned and conspicuous—orients the visitor at the entrance of each library, offering accessible public assistance and a discreet point of control.[8] These tropes have served to initiate students who might have no previous or alternate experience of a library. Even though these projects represent a new type of public school library, they have introduced students to a standard. As some participating librarians have noted, the libraries provided their students (and some parents) with their first exposure to conventional modes of research that would likely form their foundation for learning for the rest of their lives.

The library projects take their place within a reemerging consciousness in the architectural discipline that seeks to collapse the margin between progressive design and socially progressive ideals. In debates ranging across topics of public housing, public health, quality of urban life, ecologically conscious design, sheltering of homeless and international refugee populations, and artistic-political commentary, the last century reveals a frequent preoccupation with the notion that architecture is essential to social change.[9] The L!brary Initiative offers another alternative in a growing array of design programs—often spearheaded by a school, a firm, or an architect-founded nonprofit—that address social justice or humanitarian issues.

The library at Ludlow-Taylor Elementary School in Washington, D.C., opened in 2006, designed by Meditch Murphey Architects as part of the Capitol Hill Community Foundation School Libraries Project, an undertaking to overhaul school libraries in underserved neighborhoods in the nation's capital.

A Healthy Tonic

In a populist thrust, the libraries incorporate work from the hands and mouths of students. Working with design firm Pentagram and the architects responsible for the overall environments, local artists and illustrators tackled the problem of conceiving uncommon imagery that would together identify and edify. Aside from a common "L!brary" logo at the entry doorways, the graphic design at many of the libraries represents the character of a school or its neighborhood and the hand of an individual artist. Large-scale words and pictures amplify material in the books and enhance the total environment as a tool for learning. Some murals aimed to increase language arts proficiency with supergraphic text from dictionary excerpts or canonical literary references. Others documented children's aspirations and stories in multimedia.

Many of the artists and illustrators—some emerging, some established, some beloved for their *New Yorker* covers—credit the project as one of their most fulfilling, but most challenging. Many enlisted (and organized) the schools to create content, leading workshops with children selected by principals and teachers from each school, or training teachers to lead these workshops themselves in order to expand student participation. Robin Hood and the designers sought to engage teachers, students, and school administrators in envisioning the library—a donated resource some initially found challenging to manage—well before its construction. This process promoted the schools' investment, and, according to many of the artists, simultaneously inspired much of their content. Most trace the development of final pieces through an interactive process with the children and their teachers.

These artworks echo the spirit of the Works Progress Administration's Federal Art Project, which delivered the energy and tools of the arts to underserved citizens, and whose works thematically dealt with cultural issues of

Creativity- and imagination-based educational philosophies from the early twentieth century such as that of Rudolph Steiner and the Waldorf schools sought to link learning with artistic and architectural experiences.

Many L!brary Initiative participants, from former Chancellor Harold Levy to designer Michael Bierut of Pentagram, remarked on realizing that the greatest impact of the L!brary Initiative might not be on students, but on teachers.

Works Progress Administration Federal Art Project mural from the Children's Room at Queens Borough Public Library, Astoria branch, by Max Spivak. A third panel of puppets and circus characters has disappeared, along with figures of circus performers by Eugenie Gershoy. (Oil on canvas, 1935–38)

P.S. 145K students' poems on a simple scrim: "I am…grass that is sweet and sour…a tiger eating chips…sunshine chopping up darkness and stopping the light of the moon…a lazy giggle heard from a window on the street…candy in the summer…the rose that my dad gave to my mom…." Henry Myerberg and Rockwell Group intended the library to function as a gallery of students' creative work, working with Pentagram and Teachers & Writers Collaborative to design a permanent environment of text by children.

identity and moral and intellectual improvement. Several artists produced murals for New York City public buildings, including libraries and schools. Lucienne Bloch, a muralist working at the Women's House of Detention in Greenwich Village, voiced sentiments that many of the L!brary artists have echoed three-quarters of a century later:

> ...it seemed essential to bring art to the inmates by relating it closely to their own lives...I chose the only subject which would not be foreign to them—children— framed in a New York landscape of the most ordinary kind....The mural was not a foreign thing to them. In fact, in the inmates' make-believe moments, the children in the mural were adopted and named....Such response clearly reveals to what degree a mural can, aside from its artistic value, act as a healthy tonic on the lives of all of us.[10]

The implication that art for art's sake might be accessible and meaningful to a broad public falls in line with a paradoxical impulse of the L!brary Initiative to simultaneously exalt and demystify the high cultural productions of art and architecture. Through aesthetic means, practitioners have sought to render the potentially foreign space of the library familiar, while forging a cultural locus within the school. Certainly it would have been simpler, but culturally less ambitious, to donate books to schools in need or minimally renovate existing libraries. Instead, the inherent demand that the practitioner work "in terms that will stir the imagination of his public," again, echoes a civic spirit from the past:

A lost panel from the children's ward at Lincoln Hospital, New York City, by Albert Sumter Kelly, circa 1940.

> This basic policy...of painting for the people...placed painting on a level with the millions of passersby who had never thought about it before, but now began to pay attention, because it was there for them to see.[11]

Ladders (and Chutes)

> In bestowing charity, the main consideration should be to
> help those who will help themselves…the best means of
> benefiting the community is to place within its reach the
> ladders upon which the aspiring can rise—public
> institutions of various kinds, which will improve the
> general condition of the people. —Andrew Carnegie, "The
> Gospel of Wealth"

Amid the search for new ideas, an old one haunts this
Initiative, about the library as a place for advancement for
those who crave it. The story of the New York Public
Library is relevant. A philanthropic endeavor itself,
instituted with a combination of collections and bequests
from Jacob Astor, James Lenox, and former governor
Samuel Tilden, it established a public-private arrangement
to create satellite libraries throughout the boroughs. The
seed grant to New York from Andrew Carnegie, who
founded signature libraries around the world, stipulated
that the City provide branch sites and fund their
operations and maintenance. This shrewd strategy forced
all participants to take a risk bet on the odds that all would
work to succeed. Similarly, the L!brary Initiative solicits a
material investment from each participant, in the model of
"venture philanthropy" that Robin Hood has pioneered.

The New York Public Library was founded early in an era of Progressive reform that sought to enable the citizenry, often through major philanthropic projects.

The Initiative has been executed via a unique funding
and operations agreement between Robin Hood and the
City of New York that has evolved over its lifetime.
Certain standards have held throughout. The public sector
partner has matched the investment of the private sector
partner by at least double. Participating schools have
increased financial commitment over time. Syracuse
University has always underwritten some portion of
librarians' tuition for a Master of Library Science degree.
Robin Hood has brought to the table a roster of cash
donors and major product and service contributors. Every
designer involved with the project has waived fees for at
least one project and some construction management firms
have done the same. Major members of the children's book
industry have pledged generously.[12]

The challenges of the L!brary Initiative typically fall
under two categories: difficulties inevitable in design and
construction, and those specific to projects with complex
scope and sponsorship. The L!brary Initiative spans more
than one mayoral administration and school chancellery,
and the restructuring of the independent Board of
Education into a city department. Meanwhile, between
2000 and 2008, its parent organization, Robin Hood, grew
from an operating budget of approximately $4.3 million to
one above $16 million and a grantmaking budget under $13
million to one above $100 million. Aside from the
complexities and delays caused by the pursuant changes in

According to Robin Hood's Executive Director, David Saltzman, school principals are the Initiative's most important "clients." Their leadership is vital to the success of a school library.

personnel, relationships, and operating structures, the
libraries have fallen prey to more quotidian hazards, like
the global spike in construction costs caused by steel
scarcity in the years prior to the 2008 Beijing Olympics.

Robin Hood's preference for small- to medium-sized
architecture firms with a cultivated commitment to design
excellence—based on its demand for a certain level of care,
and a strategy for promoting the projects—has precluded
the repetitive mass production that would standardize
outcomes and streamline costs. Most L!brary architects,
who, along with school administrators and officials, agree
that students benefit from the exposure to thoughtfully
designed spaces, argue that this is for better and not for
worse. However, such architects do not typically court the
public sector for their primary business and have often
found the rigmarole challenging. Noted architect-activist
Hassan Fathy, in building for the rural poor in Egypt, once
described his impression that "if solving architectural
problems gives the satisfaction of climbing a mountain,
cooperating with the bureaucracy is like wading through a
bog...."[13] Nevertheless, the designers of these libraries
generally agree that the "public" aspect is the soul of the
L!brary Initiative. Designing a private school library
would hardly be as momentous. They also typically agree
that the private partner drove the quality of the L!brary
Initiative. Robin Hood's expectations were high. In
general, the participants credit the hybrid partnership
between the private and public sectors as the genius of the
Initiative.

As a civic gesture, the L!brary Initiative directly
addresses the diminishing role and quality of public space
in our culture. It does this by associating the act of
learning with safety, comfort, inspiration, stimulation,
accessibility, and beauty. It exposes children to high-
quality physical environments at a young age, promoting a
regard for them as a basis for good citizenship. The
Initiative happens to benefit several neighborhoods that
lack a public library branch. Here, the libraries have
become especially critical resources, with librarians
stocking books and encouraging programs that serve the
wider community in addition to their own students. The
first selections targeted schools in underserved
communities, but the L!brary Initiative arguably models a
culture of education that applies to all schools.

The Robin Hood L!brary Initiative furnishes certain
transferable precedents. Its educational objectives and
design guidelines are replicable. From the funding
partnership to the activities of artists and schools, it offers
a model for interdisciplinary collaboration. It sets an
example for executing vanguard architecture in the public
realm. Such aspirations translate across the globe.

However, most tools for social advocacy develop in
response to local conditions. In 1999 in New York City, 150

schools were still heated by coal and high school
graduation rates hovered around only fifty percent. In this
atmosphere, a peculiar confluence of individuals and
groups pooled their resources to overhaul what Robin
Hood often describes as the only place in a school besides
the cafeteria and washroom used by all of its students.
Many of the participants in the L!brary Initiative
acknowledge a professional and personal allegiance to New
York and an enthusiasm to serve the city in partnership
with Robin Hood. The organization's commitment to New
York City runs deep, embedded symbolically within its
own namesake:

> Gotham—which in old Anglo-Saxon means "Goats'
> Town"—was (and still is) a real village in the English
> county of Nottinghamshire, not far from Sherwood
> Forest.[14]

Notes

1. The words of a Brooklyn P.S. 106 student. L!brary Initiative promotional DVD, directed by Jim Samalis and produced by Kaleidoscope for Robin Hood, 2005.
2. See also Susan La Marca, ed., *Rethink: Ideas for Inspiring School Library Design* (Victoria, Australia: School Library Association of Victoria, 2007).
3. Henry Levin et al., "The Costs and Benefits of an Excellent Education for All of America's Children," Center for Benefit-Cost Studies of Education at Teachers College, Columbia University (January 2007): 6–12.
4. Cluster teaching arrangements, often necessary in overcrowded schools, place students in the library for a free period to relieve the regular instructor without necessarily engaging the library as an active learning resource.
5. Architectural historian Esther McCoy, on the Case Study House Program experiment in design. Esther McCoy, "Arts & Architecture Case Study Houses," *Perspecta* 15 (1975).
6. Quotes from the Editor's announcement of the Case Study House Program. *Arts & Architecture* (January 1945).
7. The period of development for the pilot libraries happened to coincide with this concept's showcasing on the world stage by the Office of Metropolitan Architecture with the Seattle Public Library, which opened in 2004.
8. Major characteristics of Carnegie libraries of New York City. Mary B. Dierickx, *The Architecture of Literacy: The Carnegie Libraries of New York City* (New York: New York City Department of General Services, 1996), 36.
9. A recent body of literature in the United States illuminates activist practices of architecture and urbanism. See, for example, Bryan Bell and Katie Wakeford, *Expanding Architecture: Design as Activism* (New York: Metropolis Books, 2008); Kate Stohr, "100 Years of Humanitarian Design," in *Design Like You Give a Damn: Architectural Responses to Humanitarian Crisis*, Architecture for Humanity (New York: Metropolis Books, 2006), 33-55; Andrea Oppenheimer Dean and Timothy Hursley, *Rural Studio: Samuel Mockbee and An Architecture of Decency* (New York: Princeton Architectural Press, 2002). The Venice Biennale 11th International Architecture Exhibition in 2008, titled "Out There: Architecture Beyond Building," directed by Aaron Betsky, dealt with "architecture beyond building to address the central issues of our society."
10. Artist Lucienne Bloch, from "Murals for Use," a 1930s essay for a proposed report to Congress to be titled "Art for the Millions" on the value of the Works Progress Administration's Federal Art Project. See also Francis V. O'Connor, ed., *Art for the Millions: Essays from the 1930s by Artists and Administrators of the WPA Federal Art Project* (Greenwich, CT: New York Graphic Society, 1973).
11. Geoffrey Norman, "The Development of American Painting," in *Art for the Millions: Essays from the 1930s by Artists and Administrators of the WPA Federal Art Project*, edited by Francis V. O'Connor (Greenwich, CT: New York Graphic Society, 1973), 50–55.
12. Robin Hood facilitated many different kinds of donations and reduced-cost products and services to the L!brary Initiative. Major children's book publishers supplemented collections. Scholastic and HarperCollins pledged one million books each, and Random House, Boyds Mill Press, Little, Brown, and World Book donated books or reduced their costs. Sagebrush and Follett provided card cataloguing, retrospective conversion for books in existing collections, and assistance with new title selection based on Department of Education curriculum standards. Custom Computer Services provided hardware and systems integration at reduced cost. Apple donated computers to some of the first participating schools. Robin Hood donor F. J. Sciame managed the construction of several libraries in a unique agreement with the Department of Education and Robin Hood. Benjamin Moore donated paint to early projects. The Rangine Corporation (Rakks) provided high-quality shelving at reduced cost. All the architects donated fees. Support came from photography agencies like Esto, Paul Warchol, and Kevin Chu/ Jessica Paul, who contributed professional images. This list of in-kind donors is not comprehensive, but is intended to outline the philanthropic scope of the Initiative.
13. Hassan Fathy, *Architecture for the Poor: An Experiment in Rural Egypt* (Chicago, University of Chicago Press, 1973), 186.
14. Edwin G. Burrows and Mike Wallace, *Gotham: A History of New York City to 1898* (New York: Oxford University Press, 1999), xii.

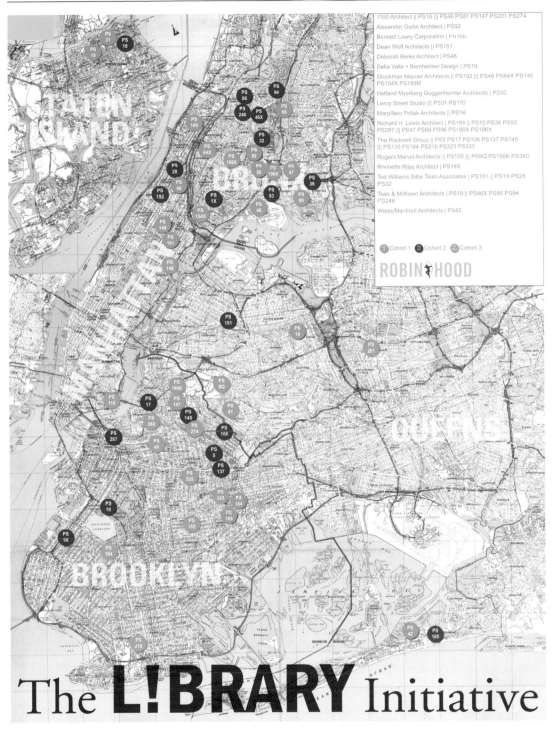

1100 Architect || PS16 ||| PS46 PS81 PS147 PS201 PS274

Alexander Gorlin Architect | PS92

Bonnett Lowry Corporation | PS165

Dean Wolf Architects || PS151

Deborah Berke Architect | PS46

Della Valle + Bernheimer Design | PS18

Gluckman Mayner Architects || PS192 ||| PS48 PS64X PS146 PS154X PS189M

Helfand Myerberg Guggenheimer Architects | PS50

Leroy Street Studio ||| PS31 PS110

Marpillero Pollak Architects | PS1K

Richard H. Lewis Architect | PS184 || PS10 PS36 PS93 PS287 ||| PS47 PS69 PS96 PS186X PS196X

The Rockwell Group || PS5 PS17 PS106 PS137 PS145 ||| PS135 PS164 PS216 PS323 PS335

Rogers Marvel Architects | PS105 ||| PS9Q PS196K PS380

Ronnette Riley Architect | PS149

Tod Williams Billie Tsien Associates | PS101 || PS1X PS28 PS32

Tsao & McKown Architects | PS19 || PS46X PS86 PS94 PS246

Weiss/Manfredi Architects | PS42

Cohort 1   Cohort 2   Cohort 3

ROBIN HOOD

The L!BRARY Initiative

Robin Hood's working map

The Libraries

The L!brary projects span the five boroughs and all school districts of the city, often located in neighborhoods facing an array of challenges. Each library is uniquely designed to facilitate performances, multi-media presentations, and other creative modes of interaction. The libraries house areas of whole class instruction performed jointly by classroom teachers and the librarian, but the rooms also accommodate small groups and individual readers, supporting the idea that learning can be both a private and a social pursuit. The presence of multiple classes and individuals engaged in a variety of noisy activities is expected to challenge children's (and teachers') preconceptions about how and where learning occurs.

Some libraries take advantage of unusual spaces in the schools. Most inhabit as prominent a location as possible inside each school, in an area once two or three contiguous classrooms, or approximately 1,700 square feet of real estate. Overcrowded schools demonstrate the desire for a library by making room for it; the conditions have occasionally caused inconvenience during the transitional process of construction and move-in, but have also heightened the significance of the library as a special instructional space.

The school buildings age from approximately a half-century to a century. Designers introduce contemporary architecture into the existing fabric while necessarily integrating infrastructure for library operations—from new radiator models that interface with century-old hot-water pipes to air conditioning that allows the library to operate in the summer to wireless internet. These multimedia rooms are equipped with smartboards, laptops, mobile listening stations, MP3 players, digital cameras, and multiple projection areas to expand the media—and mobility—of research and project development.

The libraries remain open after school hours, on weekends, and during the summer months in order to encourage the participation of parents and connect the community with the library. Some libraries hold programs that invite volunteers to read with children, or offer English language classes for parents. These design and programming decisions have amplified the library within and outside the walls of the school.

Robin Hood asked architects to create a vital center for culture within each school, with a coherent design vision that would engage children's modes of learning and perception of architecture. The project brief included areas for instruction, presentation, independent study, and general library functions: two spaces for classes of up to thirty students each, one for an adult to read to younger students and one for older students to work at desks; informal reading areas with soft, cozy chairs or other seating that would encourage students and their parents to read together; a circulation counter and librarian's desk; book shelving (to accommodate a ten-thousand-volume collection) designed proportionally to correspond to the age groups served by the distinct instructional areas; and a bank of desktop computers. In New York City, limiting the library occupancy to no more than seventy-four persons elides restrictive building codes associated with spaces for public assembly. It also roughly equals the number of two classes of thirty students each, their teachers, and library staff. Designers often responded to the mandate for a noisy, energetic room with acoustically absorbent materials. Low project cost, easy maintenance, sustainable design, and the use of well-made, durable materials and products have been encouraged in the L!brary Initiative. Designs have considered the scale and perspective of the child, but have also addressed the need for organization of elementary school students in a learning environment.

The following pages spotlight ideas discovered in the process of designing libraries for public schools across the five boroughs. While every school tells an important story, the twelve case studies here represent the broader sample. They also catalogue distinct aesthetic visions for educational environments.

The Bronx

P.S. 1
Courtlandt
335 East 152nd Street

P.S. 32
Belmont School
690 East 183rd Street

P.S. 36
Union Port
1070 Castle Hill Avenue

P.S. 46
Edgar Allen Poe
279 East 196th Street

P.S. 47
John Randolph
1794 East 172nd Street

P.S. 48
Joseph R. Drake
1290 Spofford Avenue

C.S. 50
Clara Barton
1550 Vyse Avenue

P.S. 64
Pura Belpre
1425 Walton Avenue

P.S. 69
The New Vision School
560 Theriot Avenue

P.S. 86
Kings Bridge Heights
2756 Reservoir Avenue

C.S. 92
700 East 179th Street

P.S. 93
Albert G. Oliver
1535 Story Avenue

P.S. 94
Kings College
3530 Kings College Place

P.S. 96
Richard Rodgers
650 Waring Avenue

P.S. 154
Jonathan D. Hyatt
333 East 135th Street

P.S. 186
Walter J. Damrosch
750 Jennings Street

P.S. 196
1250 Ward Avenue

P.S. 246
Poe Center
2641 Grand Concourse

The New Vision School
560 Theriot Avenue
Soundview

Grades Served
Pre-K–5,
Special Education

Student Enrollment
580

Library Opened
2009

Architectural and
Graphic Design
Richard H. Lewis Architect
Christoph Niemann
Pentagram Design

Construction
TNS Contruction

THIS PAGE AND OPPOSITE:
Before and after

Embracing the library's symbolic potential, principal Alan Cohen chose to locate it in the most thought-provoking site possible. Displacing his own office and those of the rest of the administration, he advocated situating the library in a horseshoe plan around the stair at the main entrance to the school. Students walking into the building must enter up "through" the library to the main floor, forcing them to confront the spectacle of the library coming in, going out, and passing through. The new library is the latest piece in a school makeover that from 2003 to 2008 has doubled enrollment, added the fifth grade and two full-time pre-kindergarten classes, and raised performance dramatically. In 2003, thirty percent of fourth-grade students met the city average in reading scores. As of 2008, that figure climbed to sixty-seven percent. The school's overall reading scores fall in the top quarter, with math scores in the top tenth. The principal credits the support of a tightly knit, education-oriented community of families, and sees the "artful, quirky" new library as its visual expression.

The architects felt that reinventing the library was a complicated mandate in the case of children who lack any exposure to the institution. Richard Lewis' firm defined an approach to designing the public school library in a total of ten Initiative libraries by quoting the precedent of the grand public reading room, employing a historical interpretation of the traditional mission to educate, uplift, and empower citizens with literacy, education, and exposure to the world. The library ought to take its visitors seriously; neither architecture nor art should condescend to the young. High-quality milled casework or metal shelving and Modern-period furniture reflect a collage of design components intended to build a dossier of "classics" equal to those on the bookshelves. Contemporary New York artists and Pentagram Design provided murals for the walls of each library designed by this firm.

"You know when you have a wildest dream and it comes true?" Principal Alan Cohen acknowledges the competitive process to participate in an Initiative that had already gained recognition by the time his school was selected. He wanted a library made for children and their parents, and he says the architects listened thoughtfully.

from Long Walk to Freedom by Nelson Mandela

PREVIOUS SPREAD AND THIS PAGE: Haller shelving system from Switzerland, "Seven" chair from Denmark by Arne Jacobsen, and "Orange Slice" chairs from the Netherlands by Pierre Paulin

Christoph Niemann animated books to illustrate the Dewey Decimal system for cataloguing subject matter.

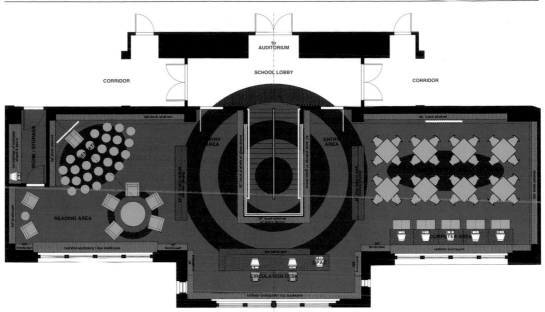

**Public School 69
Floor Plan**

A single color sets apart an experience. The linoleum floor bullseye (Robin Hood's logo) extends the zone of the library horizontally and vertically.

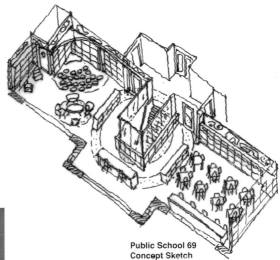

**Public School 69
Concept Sketch**

Custom light fixtures designed and fabricated by Paul Merwin of Fabulux, Inc. in the Brooklyn Navy Yard

PS 32

Belmont School
690 East 183rd Street
Belmont

Grades Served
K–5,
Special Education

Student Enrollment
801

Library Opened
2004

Architectural and
Graphic Design
Tod Williams Billie Tsien
  Architects
Pentagram Design

Construction
F.J. Sciame Construction

This early 1900s school building is affectionately called the "castle of learning" by principal Esther Schwartz and librarian Maureen Hurley. Gargoyles at the eaves of its steeply-pitched roofs, wide hallways and foyers, and high ceilings supported by cast iron columns form the backdrop to a contemporary library that invokes the fantasy of another time or place. A starry night sky—a dark blue ceiling punctured by points of light, with stalactite fixtures inspired by the architects' encounter with Isamu Noguchi—unifies the cozy alcoves formed by bookshelves below. Billie Tsien has remarked on the private experience of a library, the power of reading as a refuge or escape. This library extends the flight of fancy generated by the "castle" itself, reminiscent of Noguchi's own dreamlike stage sets.

Denis Diderot's eighteenth-century *Encyclopédie*—a work conspicuous for fermenting a new intellectual and social consciousness in the West ("the Enlightenment")—provided the concept for the library's graphic imagery. Concerned with decorating the walls with pictures meaningful to children, the architects credit the primacy and relevance of this book to Enlightenment philosophical ideals that were, in turn, fundamental to libraries. They cite its combined scientific and artful approach and the sheer beauty of its line drawings. The images register other landmarks familiar to the students: the Bronx Zoo and New York Botanical Garden two blocks away, both institutions with a close relationship to P.S. 32.

From the vestibule, a large corner window announces the library, three former classrooms on the third floor.

THIS PAGE: *Littering a library with fine accents. Lunella "mushroom cap" cushions from Baleri Italia over V'soske rugs and cork floors, Aalto chairs and tables and Eames tables from Herman Miller.*

Tod Williams Billie Tsien
Architects selected different
illustrations for the four libraries
in their portfolio.

At P.S. 1X (shown here) and
P.S. 28M drawings were
printed on window shades.

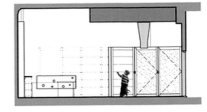

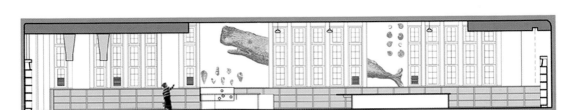

LIBRARY INITIATIVE
PUBLIC SCHOOL 32
690 E. 183RD STREET
BRONX, NY 10458

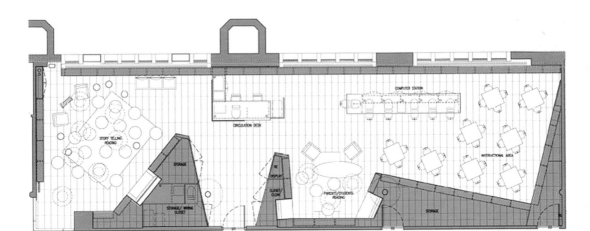

The Akari paper lantern formed the basis of the traveling exhibition Quiet Light that Tod Williams Billie Tsien Architects designed and curated for the Noguchi Foundation after the artist's death. He examined the form throughout his career. Its functionality and affordability contributed to its popularity (and criticism of the artist). The architects chose to quote the luminous object in a version that would scale the library to the size of children. "We were lucky to meet and tour his studio. We came to know the lamps quite well and were always amazed by how they were able to give light and be sculptural presences at the same time."—Billie Tsien

Brooklyn

P.S. 1
The Bergen School
309 47th Street

P.S. 5
Dr. Ronald McNair
820 Hancock Street

P.S. 10
Magnet School of Math,
Science, and Design
511 7th Avenue

P.S. 17
Henry D. Woodworth
208 North 5th Street

P.S. 46
Edward C. Blum
100 Clermont Avenue

P.S. 106
Edward Everett Hale School
1314 Putnam Avenue

P.S. 135
Sheldon A. Brookner
684 Linden Boulevard

P.S. 137
Rachel Jean Mitchell
121 Saratoga Avenue

P.S. 145
Andrew Jackson
100 Noll Street

P.S. 147
Isaac Remsen
325 Bushwick Avenue

P.S. 164
Caesar Rodney
4211 14th Avenue

P.S. 165
Ida Posner
76 Lott Avenue

P.S. 184
Newport
273 Newport Street

P.S. 196
Ten Eyck
207 Bushwick Avenue

P.S. 216
Arturo Toscanini
350 Avenue X

P.S. 274
Kosciusko
800 Bushwick Avenue

P.S. 287
Bailey K. Ashford
50 Navy Street

P.S. 323
210 Chester Street

P.S. 335
Granville Woods
130 Rochester Avenue

P.S. 380
John Wayne
370 Marcy Avenue

PS 1

The Bergen School
309 47th Street
Sunset Park

Grades Served
Pre-K–5,
Special Education

Student Enrollment
1,000

Library Opened
2004

Architectural and
Graphic Design
Marpillero Pollak Architects
Pentagram Design

Construction
F.J. Sciame Construction

The Brooklyn-Queens Expressway and local commercial and light industrial zoning physically divides the Sunset Park neighborhood of P.S. 1. The rift in the urban fabric has allowed some unsavory businesses to flourish and compromised the safety of the neighborhood. Over ninety-five percent of the thousand mostly immigrant Spanish-speaking students of P.S. 1 live below the poverty line, and working parents rely on the school year-round for part of the care of their children. Librarian Nuala Pacheco credits high parent involvement under these stressed circumstances with encouraging students to borrow books and supporting her attempts to collaborate with the public library two blocks away. Students in the pre-kindergarten through fifth grade school visit the school library in class groups at least every other week and students learning English as a second language meet there once a week.

In contrast to the urban character of the neighborhood, the P.S. 1 library is a microcosm of order, with "streets" and "squares" and zones for a range of activities. Linda Pollak described four impressions that emerged as she and her partner Sandro Marpillero visited previously built Initiative libraries: the quantity of furniture was dense for the size of the rooms, the relatively small spaces contained several simultaneous functions, the library had the capacity to physically impact the geography of an entire school, and the schools might be meaningfully involved in the design process. Marpillero Pollak Architects responded to these perceptions with a participatory design process and a landscape of architectural and urbanistic components that operate at many scales, from the furniture to the room to the school to the city.

Bank Street-educated librarian and former architect Nuala Pacheco attributed her high level of input in the design process in part to working with a team that included a female architect. P.S. 1K architect Linda Pollak, like Ronnette Riley, Billie Tsien, Marion Weiss, Kathryn Dean, Deborah Berke and the many women on the L!brary design teams—all of whom have changed the landscape of the profession—recast the image of the design process for an important public: educators and children.

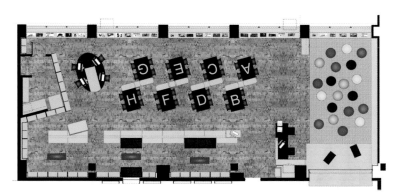

Fixed desk-height kiosks provide order to the instructional area by anchoring and supplying electrical power to the milled wood desks that cluster flexibly around them. The cork floor absorbs extra noise in the room. According to librarian Nuala Pacheco, the kids say the library "smells of wood."

ABOVE: *Component pieces are mobile and allow flexible reconfiguration. Level changes, materials, lighting, and furniture establish microenvironments.*

A bench outside provides a physical transition into the library from the "street." The library's interior floor area was sacrificed to create a public space in the common corridor. Schoolchildren gather here, a staff member has used the furniture for physical therapy, and one security guard performs daily namaaz in the space.

ABOVE: Lunella mushroom-cap stools over a Chilewich fabric mat on the floor mirror the colored Plexiglas lenses and white Jasper Morrison spherical lights that penetrate the perforated metal ceiling above.

LEFT: Students created artwork for permanent display in the windows.

PS 106

Edward Everett Hale School
1314 Putnam Avenue
Bushwick

Grades Served
Pre-K–5,
Special Education

Student Enrollment
596

Library Opened
2004

Architectural and
Graphic Design
Henry Myerberg and
Rockwell Group
Dave Johnson and
Teachers & Writers
Collaborative
Pentagram Design

Construction
F.J. Sciame Construction

*ABOVE: The central stair
leads to a skyline view
described by Principal Flores
as a metaphor for success.*

Principal for over a decade of a school in a high-crime area whose previous library was little more than a storeroom of books, Robert Flores noted parents' discomfort with sending their children to the public library. Gang problems and neighborhood safety concerns hindered P.S. 106 from relying on the small neighborhood branch to expand research and educational projects. For a school attended by generations of families, Principal Flores and architect Henry Myerberg offered a surprise destination. Sidestepping a L!brary Initiative tactic to site new facilities in prominent ground-floor locations, they took advantage of an unused attic gym with dramatic clerestory windows. The new design situated risers below the central window to form a theater. Hundreds of thought bubbles hover on the walls and ceiling above, asking the visitor questions such as "When they made the first clock, how did they know what time it was?" and "Why do we go to war to have peace?"

Henry Myerberg's practice has long engaged the problem of shifting the paradigm of the library from what he calls a "warehouse" of information to a "marketplace" for the creation and exchange of ideas. His partnership with Robin Hood began with a prototype library at the Beginning With Children Charter School in Brooklyn. Later, he organized design teams and spearheaded the collaborative development of the architectural guidelines for the L!brary Initiative, articulating the cost-benefit ratio of the rejuvenated library in terms of the value of improving five percent of a school's real estate to serve one hundred percent of its students and community.

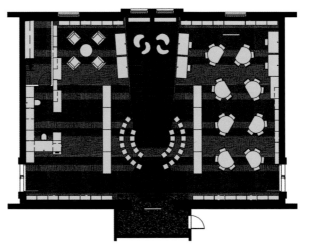

*Exclaiming the importance
of the library by demarcating
the amphitheater and stage.
Banded blue carpet tiles
express the Fibonacci number
series (1,1,2,3,5).*

Before and after

ABOVE: *Punctuation to sit on and walk through. The glass vision panels in the doors reflect the Spanish- and English-speaking population of the school.*

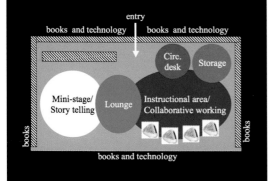

Henry Myerberg worked on eleven Initiative libraries in various collaborative partnerships (five while at Rockwell Group that include the project at P.S. 106K) and facilitated the pro bono involvement of engineers and other consultants. Architectural goals in these projects have included flexibility of layout, affordability, ease of construction and maintenance, and principles of environmental sustainability. Most of them reflect design collaborations on interiors with Karen Davidov and on furniture and millwork with Peter Danko, who fabricated cost-efficient modular shelving, reconfigurable worktables on casters, and chairs with backs and seats made of recycled seatbelts.

entry

books and technology   books and technology

Circ. desk   Storage

Mini-stage/ Story telling   Lounge   Instructional area/ Collaborative working

books

books

books and technology

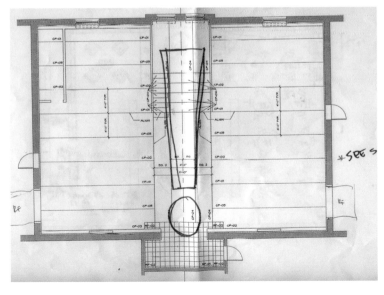

American author Edward Everett Hale might have liked to see poetry generated at his namesake school. Workshops between P.S. 106K students and poet Dave Johnson unearthed most of the questions on the walls, based on selections from Pablo Neruda's Book of Questions. The irresistible assignment also captivated members of the Robin Hood community; one L!brary Initiative donor takes credit for the question "Why do we have to get married when we grow up?"

Manhattan

P.S. 28
Wright Brothers
475 West 155th Street

P.S. 46
Arthur Tappan
2987 Frederick Douglas Boulevard

P.S. 101
Andrew Draper
141 East 111th Street

P.S. 110
Florence Nightingale School
285 Delancey Street

P.S. 146
Anna M. Short
421 East 106th Street

P.S. 149
Sojourner Truth
41 West 117th Street

P.S. 189
2580 Amsterdam Avenue

P.S. 192
Jacob H. Schiff
500 West 138th Street

PS 189

2580 Amsterdam Avenue
Washington Heights

Grades Served
Pre-K–5,
Special Education

Student Enrollment
1,078

Library Opened
2008

Architectural and
Graphic Design
Gluckman Mayner Architects
2x4

Construction
Iannelli Construction

P.S. 189 students accustomed to assignment-based classroom instruction welcomed the new mode of study: autonomous, self-directed research. For instance, in a 2008 project on presidential candidates Barack Obama and John McCain culminated in a mock election. In this crowded school over ten blocks away from the closest public library branch, librarian Margaret Goulet has focused on demystifying the structure, operations, and resources of a library to many children who have never been inside one. She has oriented the elementary school's nearly eleven hundred students to the new facility with the goal of preparing them to navigate any library. As she puts it, even a library with books flying across the sky uses the Dewey Decimal system.

Years of work with artist Dan Flavin before his death in 1996 inspired architect Richard Gluckman to recast the typical fluorescent light fixture found in public schools. A progression of sculptural "bird" postures borrows mathematical ideas from a chronophotographical analysis of bird flight by nineteenth-century French scientist Etienne-Jules Marey and British photographer Eadweard Muybridge. Sheet metal "wings" span across tube lights in the shape of open books, mounted at fixed intervals in plan, at varying heights from the plane of the "sky," and open at alternating angles. The consideration of the whole environment for a student's encounter with books reflects Gluckman Mayner's extensive background in museum design, representing years of investigating how a viewer contemplates a work of art—in this case, the book.

The new library

The former library

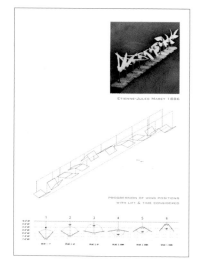

ABOVE: *An extensive process of mocking up the light fixture rendered a flock of books that flies through a digitally printed sky.*

LEFT: *Series of eleven statuettes representing the flight of the pigeon by Etienne-Jules Marey. (Positive photographic plaque from the Cinémathèque française collection of apparatuses.) Gluckman Mayner Architects' analysis of wing positions.*

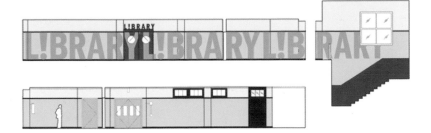

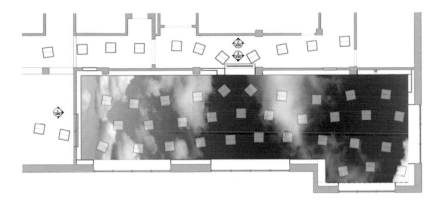

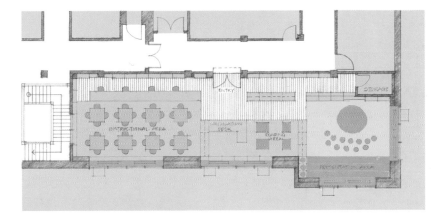

According to librarian Margaret Goulet, students have to work on assignments in class, but in the library, they get to select books themselves. She tells her students that even on a rainy day, she has a blue sky.

As an early 1970s graduate of Syracuse University, Richard Gluckman cultivated an interest in social activism, which, in the pre-Reagan United States, often turned architects to public housing projects. Gluckman Mayner Architects designed six Initiative libraries, beginning with this one, at P.S. 192 in Manhattan.

PS 110

Florence Nightingale School
285 Delancey Street
Lower East Side

Grades Served
Pre-K–5,
Special Education

Student Enrollment
469

Library Opened
2008

Architectural and
Graphic Design
Leroy Street Studio
Hester Street Collaborative
Pentagram Design

Construction
Champion Construction

Leroy Street Studio founders Marc Turkel and Morgan Hare appreciated the L!brary Initiative's focus on design as a rubric of engagement for activists. In 2002, they founded the Hester Street Collaborative to help non-architects design and build projects in their neighborhoods. They emphasized their concern that design typically takes a backseat to the disciplines of planning and education as arenas where low-income communities have the ability to advocate for or shape the built environment.

Workshops at P.S. 110 between students, teachers, and Hester Street Collaborative produced a permanent library installation of student artwork inspired by titles in the collection. This background celebration of books was a natural tactic for Audrey Fraenkel, a librarian of nine years who never had trouble getting children to come to the library. She and her own children attended P.S. 110, like a number of other teachers in this school that Manhattan real-estate advertisements describe as "one of the best-kept secrets of the Lower East Side." Generations of families have formed a tight core of relationships in this downtown neighborhood that has shifted demographics in recent history, simultaneously attracting a variety of new immigrants and increased gentrification. Leroy Street Studio's proposal for ramps and portholes in the new library—elements that offer children alternate physical points of view—suggest a positive architectural metaphor for changing perspectives.

The Williamsburg Bridge as a front porch

LEFT: The double-sided shelving system hangs by cables and nautical hardware.

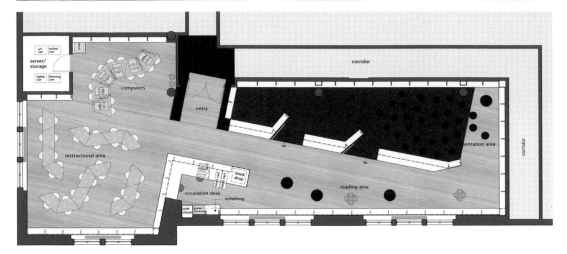

*Freestanding trapezoidal
desks in serpentine configurations accommodate group
work.*

*Circles float throughout the
room, in portholes
perforating the central
hanging bookcase, custom
yellow lighting baffles in the
ceiling, glass panels in the
entry doors, seating cushions
in the storytelling area, and
openings in the entry portal.*

Queens

P.S. 9
58-74 57th Street

P.S. 19
Marino Jeantet School
98-02 Roosevelt Avenue

P.S. 42
R. Vernam School
488 Beech 66th Street

P.S. 81
Jean Paul Richter
559 Cypress Avenue

P.S. 105
The Bay School
420 Beach 51st Street

P.S. 151
Mary D. Carter
50-05 31st Avenue

P.S. 201
Kissena
65-11 155 Street

PS 105

The Bay School
420 Beach 51st Street
Far Rockaway

Grades Served
Pre-K–5,
Special Education

Student Enrollment
911

Library Opened
2004

Architectural and
Graphic Design
Rogers Marvel Architects
Pentagram Design

Construction
F.J. Sciame Construction

P.S. 105 is a safe place for many students living in the adjacent low-income housing projects. Principal Laurie Shapiro walks to the street corner every morning to fetch children who might otherwise skip school, and librarian Helen Feldman-Goldstein lives in the neighborhood and has taught at P.S. 105 for over twenty years. After the library was instituted, children were spotted reading while waiting in line for the bathroom. Library books went missing, to the delight of the staff, who suspected the children were stealing them to read at home.

Rogers Marvel Architects concerned themselves with the idea of an oasis that could shelter children from the stresses of their lives outside, and encourage them to relax and get lost in a good book. Orange and pink pastels alternating down the length of the room set a tone reminiscent of a beach—a landscape geographically close enough to give P.S. 105 its namesake, but atmospherically far from the troubled neighborhood. Through a hierarchy of spatial experiences, the architects conceived of many rooms of different scales within the larger library, some orchestrated with color, some carved out of the architecture.

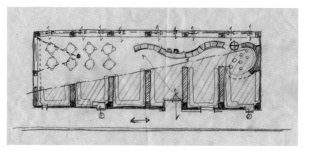

Making space with color. Bays formed from ceiling-height bookshelves against the wall, low shelves projecting into the room, and hovering ceiling planes establish a variety of interiors. The lower shelves allow the librarian a clean line of sight and the piers form a protected "back."

Seating nooks and other niches diversify interior spaces to the scale of a child. P.S. 105Q has expanded to incorporate a middle school in recent years. Ms. Feldman-Goldstein has promoted buddy reading programs and lunchtime tutoring where older children and younger children work together in the library.

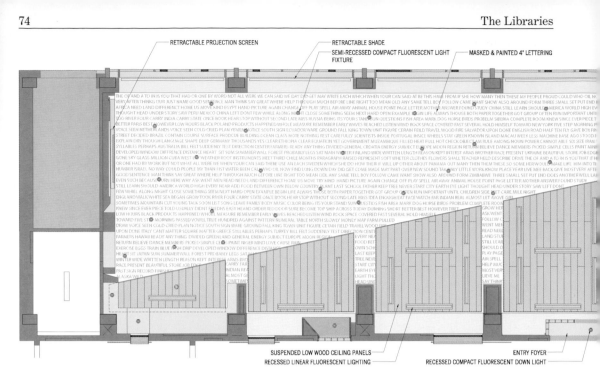

RETRACTABLE PROJECTION SCREEN
RETRACTABLE SHADE
SEMI-RECESSED COMPACT FLUORESCENT LIGHT FIXTURE
MASKED & PAINTED 4' LETTERING

SUSPENDED LOW WOOD CEILING PANELS
RECESSED LINEAR FLUORESCENT LIGHTING
ENTRY FOYER
RECESSED COMPACT FLUORESCENT DOWN LIGHT

A Robin Hood staff member contributed an idea for a game embedded in this library. A matrix of questions stripes the ceiling. The answers float down the vertical surfaces. The only way to match the questions to the answers is to read the books in the library.

As Michael Winerip reported in the New York Times, February 23, 2005, "It is a very big deal, the new library at P.S. 105. A new library feeds a boy's dreams. 'When this library first opened,' said Isaiah Ross, a fifth grader, 'I promised myself I'd read every dinosaur book here.'" Winerip pinpointed a critical matter: "When a library is the most beautiful room a child has ever seen, it sends a message."

RETRACTABLE PROJECTION SCREEN
TRACK LIGHTING

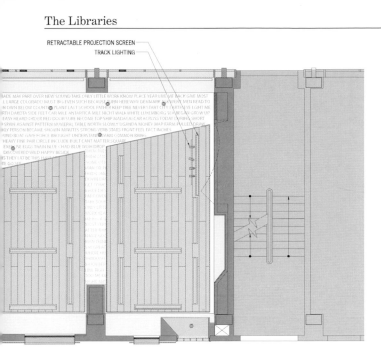

REFLECTED CEILING PLAN

PS 19

Marino Jeantet School
98-02 Roosevelt Avenue
Corona

Grades Served
K–5,
Special Education

Student Enrollment
1,968

Library Opened
2002

Architectural and
Graphic Design
Tsao & McKown Architects
Pentagram Design

Construction
F.J. Sciame Construction

Maxine Rappaport, a librarian of twenty years and long-time neighborhood resident, works in one of the smallest libraries in one of the highest-population schools participating in the L!brary Initiative. Her custom approach to each student has encouraged significant independent learning and research in the P.S. 19 library and built important community partnerships, especially with the nearby public library branch. One of her old students often comes back to visit because P.S. 19 has the best Braille collection of children's books in the neighborhood.

Tsao & McKown Architects expanded the limited footprint of the library through the use of screens and scrims, deepening the landscape by creating foreground and background, and framed views from protected interiors. Architect Zack McKown remembers discovering Billie Holliday in an audio library in seventh grade. He linked the introversive library and privacy of one's thoughts to the development of one's own vision—the development of an artists' sensibility—recalling the essay "Self-Reliance," in which Ralph Waldo Emerson wrote, "To believe your own thought, to believe that what is true for you in your private heart is true for all men—that is genius." Besides designing a library that would be affordable, easy to build, and environmentally sustainable, the architects envisioned a place that would act as a scaffolding, to be literally and metaphorically completed by the students' work.

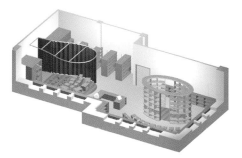

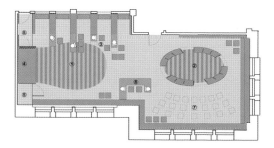

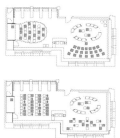

Librarian Maxine Rappaport brags about her summer students. "They don't even know it's time to go home. They don't even ask me."

The fire-retardant curtain—an element from Calvin Tsao's background in theater—encloses a room where librarian Maxine Rappaport and her students teleconferenced with NASA.

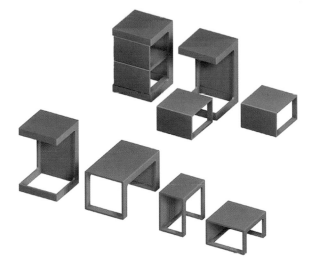

From the industrial design segment of the architects' diverse portfolio of experience came the prototype development for cost-efficient, modular, multi-purpose children's furniture.

PS
19

Marino Jeantet School
98–02 Roosevelt Avenue
Corona

Grades Served
K–5,
Special Education

Student Enrollment
1,968

Learning Garden
Opened 2003

Architectural and
Graphic Design
Ken Smith Landscape
  Architect
Pentagram Design

Construction
New York Restoration Project

P.S. 19 teacher Charis Stozek runs programs in science and reading in the learning garden, independent of the library. Every year during Earth Week, the school's two thousand students, including fourteen kindergarten classes, participate in nature scavenger hunts and recycling activities. April is poetry month; students write in the garden and teachers hold read-alouds.

Landscape Architect Ken Smith learned of Robin Hood when he began receiving persistent requests to improve a schoolyard at a L!brary Initiative site. This was the Initiative's first experiment in outdoor learning environments for a school with very little outdoor space. At the time, it was the second largest elementary school in the country. After a morning visit to P.S. 19, Smith sketched five low-cost concepts and turned in a proposal the next day that would unconventionally deploy a palette of common prefabricated materials in a manner that could be copied at other school sites. He credits the Robin Hood staff for providing the necessary organization in the field to maximize his pro bono effort and reduce his overhead expense. The project happened quickly, and volunteers from the school, the community, and Robin Hood did all the planting and installations.

He isolated maintenance and upgrade as the greatest challenges in designing a schoolyard. The scrim on the chain-link fence came loose eventually. The Bird and Butterfly Garden fared better, due to the school's continued attention and upkeep. Garden work has served as a gathering point for the primarily Spanish-speaking neighborhood—teachers and parents typically work with the children to care for it during school hours. They weed, plant bulbs in the fall, and make scarecrows as necessary.

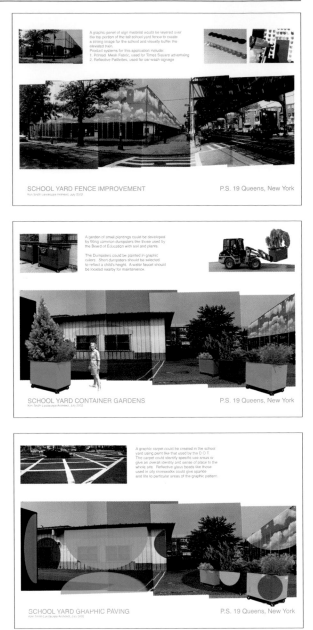

SCHOOL YARD FENCE IMPROVEMENT   P.S. 19 Queens, New York

SCHOOL YARD CONTAINER GARDENS   P.S. 19 Queens, New York

SCHOOL YARD GRAPHIC PAVING   P.S. 19 Queens, New York

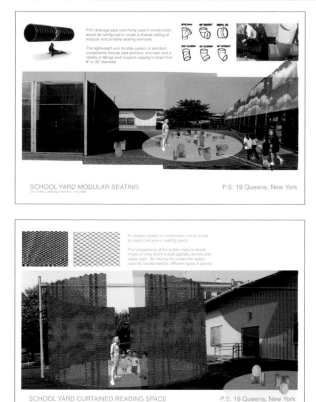

From the School Yard Improvements proposal by Ken Smith Landscape Architect, July 2002:

This study includes five low-cost school yard improvements.

Each idea is based on transforming a commercially available product for a new use.

Through use of everyday objects children will make connections to the outside world.

The transformation of these objects will encourage creative thought.

These ideas serve as prototypes for addressing typical school yard problems at variable sites.

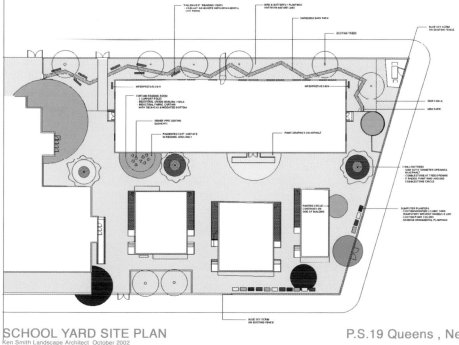

SCHOOL YARD SITE PLAN
Ken Smith Landscape Architect October 2002

P.S.19 Queens , New York

R. Vernam School
488 Beech 66th Street
Arverne

Grades Served
K–8,
Special Education

Student Enrollment
782

Library Opened
2002

Architectural and
Graphic Design
Weiss/Manfredi Architecture/
 Landscape/Urbanism
Pentagram Design

Construction
F.J. Sciame Construction

Since the library at P.S. 42 was built, the school grew from an elementary to a middle school, adding grades six through eight. Principal Riva Madden describes the school's need to retool the resource, including the book collection, to meet the pedagogical needs of older children. The expansion rendered certain design elements especially critical: a scrim that forms a semi-private enclosure, rolling book stacks that increase the useable floor area, and large mobile bean bag ottomans that serve as both comfortable chairs and space dividers.

Architects Marion Weiss and Michael Manfredi reviewed the initial project site—a row of classrooms on the fourth floor—and argued to locate the library on the ground floor instead, in a prominent location near the building entry. They describe this as the first critical design decision, necessary to anchor the library in the collective consciousness of the school, and worth displacing one of two gyms. According to Riva Madden, this convenient and secure location has allowed visitors from the community—"the regulars"—to access the library. It also freed classroom space upstairs for the eventual growth of the school.

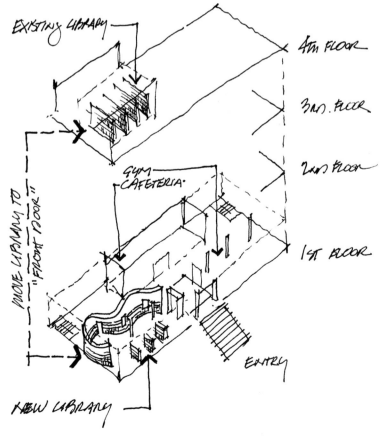

The figural wall of books defined the interior and exterior form of the library and expanded the perimeter of the open plan from fifty to ninety feet in length. The architects' desire to "make the books spatial" and allow the wall to "wander out of the sightline" challenged institutional paradigms, as did the warmth of wood along the curves, the bold red carpet and furniture, and the softening of overhead fluorescent lighting with translucent baffles.

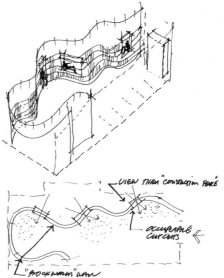

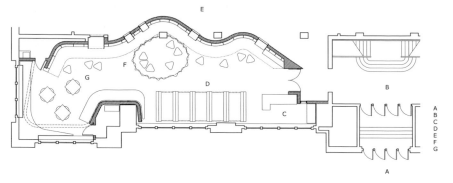

A	BUILDING ENTRY
B	FOYER
C	LIBRARIANS WORK AREA
D	DEPLOYABLE BOOKSHELVES
E	CORRIDOR
F	STORYTELLING CURTAIN
G	ROLLING BEAN BAG CHAIRS

LIBRARY - CONFIGURED FOR INDIVIDUAL STUDY

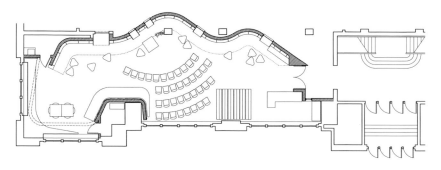

LIBRARY - CONFIGURED FOR LARGE GATHERINGS

As part of a global youth connection, two fifth-grade classes at P.S. 42Q partnered with two classes in Cameroon. Students researched the western African nation in the library. They wrote to students there and spoke directly with them via conference call. They learned about the civil unrest in Cameroon when their pen pals had to cancel a video conference.

Staten Island

P.S. 16
John J. Driscoll School
80 Monroe Avenue

P.S. 18
John Greenleaf Whittier School
221 Broadway

P.S. 31
William T. Davis
55 Layton Avenue

John J. Driscoll School
80 Monroe Avenue
Tompkinsville

Grades Served
Pre-K–5,
Special Education

Student Enrollment
1,024

Library Opened
2004

Architectural and
Graphic Design
1100 Architect
Pentagram Design

Construction
F.J. Sciame Construction

With at least fifteen languages represented in the student body, P.S. 16 is the most multicultural school in Staten Island. Librarian Viki Tsougros faced the challenge of supplementing Robin Hood's starter collection of books with titles for English language learners. Her Spanish collection for the pre-kindergarten through fifth-grade age range exceeds that of the local public library branch, especially in non-fiction. The library hosts reading and literacy workshops for students and parents, computer classes, and lunchtime professional development sessions for teachers. 13,000 books are checked out per year, and students are required to develop and hone universally applicable research skills.

She credits the central "bookworm" with forming a room where children feel comfortable. 1100 Architect proposed a sculptural system of horizontal planes above the continuous vinyl floor to emphasize lightness and the flow of space. Its permeability allows the librarian to monitor distant activity from the circulation desk. The curves of the object divide the space into distinct student work areas, while the structure holds enough books to free the perimeter from the visual and physical burden of shelving that is densely packed with books. In a process of design modeling and testing in the field, 1100 Architect devised a logical process for fabricating multiple serpentine objects similar to the one at P.S. 16, while still accommodating a custom approach to each. The system of components was assembled at each of five Brooklyn libraries later designed by the architects.

An explosion of primary colors against a white backdrop: verbs on utilitarian sliding closet doors, a seamless vinyl floor, laminate plywood Rakks shelving (much of which was donated by the Runyine Corporation) and spray-painted polyurethane foam cushions, beneath the floating Barrisol overhead light fixtures.

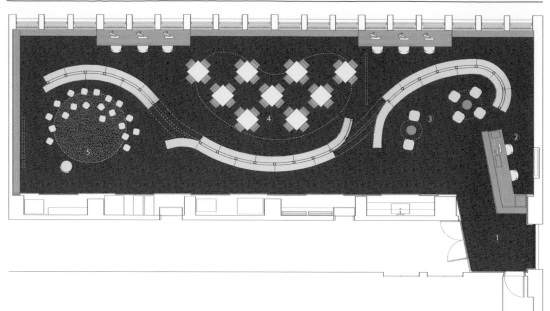

1 ENTRY

2 CIRCULATION

3 FREE FORM READING AREA

4 INSTRUCTIONAL AREA

5 PRESENTATION AREA

The best response to a custom library is a custom approach to learning. Librarian Viki Tsougros enticed an autistic child in the special education program into the library by letting him run around inside. The child returned often, and his classroom teacher rewarded his daily work by sending him to the library. Years later, he still visits the library every day, even when the facility is not open. According to his friend Ms. Tsougros, "The library is closed, but not for you."

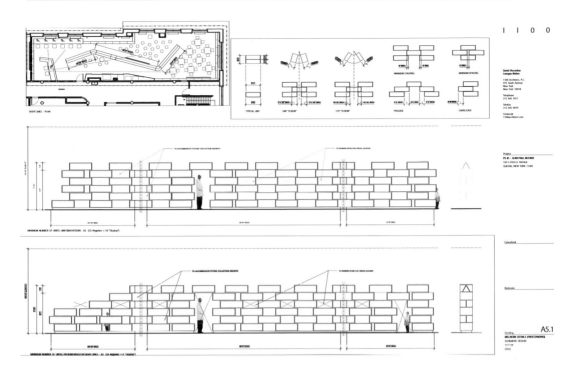

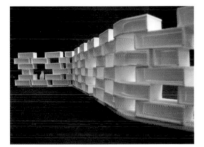

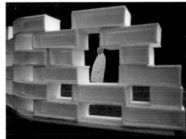

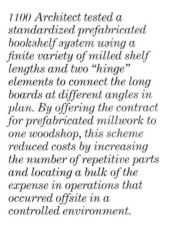

1100 Architect tested a standardized prefabricated bookshelf system using a finite variety of milled shelf lengths and two "hinge" elements to connect the long boards at different angles in plan. By offering the contract for prefabricated millwork to one woodshop, this scheme reduced costs by increasing the number of repetitive parts and locating a bulk of the expense in operations that occurred offsite in a controlled environment.

The standardized "bookworm" at P.S. 274K

PS 18

John Greenleaf Whittier
School
221 Broadway
West Brighton

Grades Served
Pre-K–5,
Special Education

Student Enrollment
579

Library Opened
2002

Architectural and
Graphic Design
Della Valle Bernheimer
Pentagram Design

Construction
AWL Industries

P.S. 18 sits across from a low-income housing project in an economically depressed neighborhood. In recent years, the school has weathered gang shootings and drug activity just outside its doors. P.S. 18 serves as a universal feeding center for students, open in the summer to any children under the age of eighteen. Books in the old library were so out of date that the principal closed the facility.

For the new library, Della Valle Bernheimer proposed the imagery of a subway car, one of New York's most recognizable icons and spatial experiences. Window slots at the height of a child's eyes puncture the shiny wrapper in the hallway. Large pivoting panels subvert their expectations of entry doors. The book stacks mimic the compression of an underground train car.

The library is open for story hour after school and students protested when it had to close for a short period for computer repairs. The library has become integrated in the life of the school, and was informally named for beloved custodian Wayne Derrick (known to everyone as "Chops"). Librarian Maryanna Crawford noted the impact of a unique design on the self-esteem of children—and teachers—who rarely encounter the finer experiences in life. Namely, it created the sense that "we were special."

Discovering the library
through sliver windows and
from thresholds between
distinct work environments

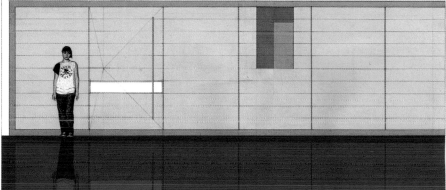

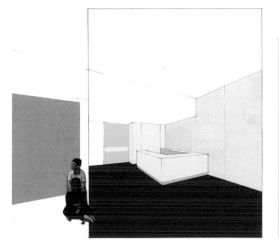

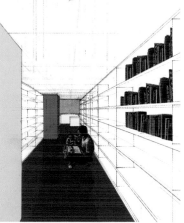

The original design called for interactive moveable parts that pull down, out, or apart to reveal hidden surprises. The project survived a value-engineering exercise that eliminated a pull-down stage behind closet doors in the style of a Murphy bed, and replaced chalkboard and whiteboard desktop scratch surfaces with linoleum. Full height stainless steel-faced cabinets line the back of the stacks to provide general storage.

OPPOSITE PAGE: With two public access doors and the circulation desk at only one end, the librarian must proactively maintain operational control, aided by a highly ordered space and intact lines of sight down the length of the library.

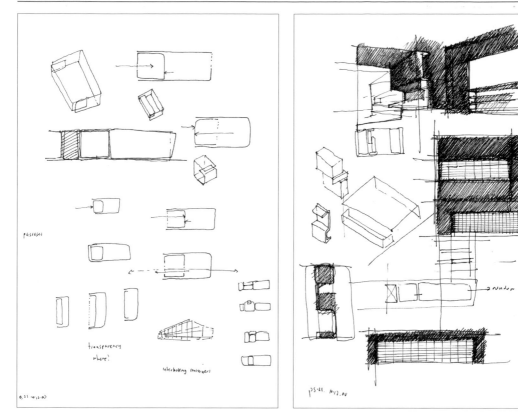

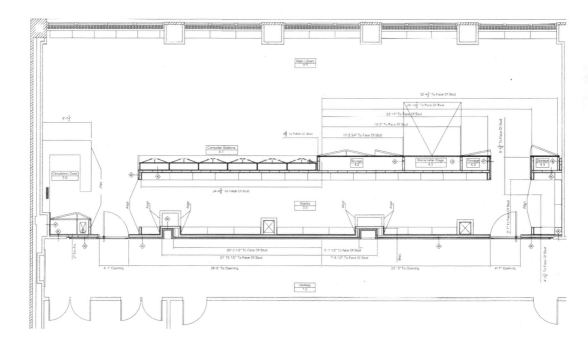

The Art of the Library

Works Progress Administration artist James Michael Newell conceived a "series of murals describing the growth of western civilization" for a Bronx school library:

> My first consideration in approaching the work of decorating the library of the Evander Childs High School in New York City was its physical dimensions which are approximately one hundred by sixty feet. The space to be decorated, except for pilasters dividing the long wall, presented a continuous stretch about eight feet high around three sides of the room above the wood paneling and bookshelves. Murals for a room of such proportions must be planned to an over-life-size scale and must be bold in design if their meaning is to reach the students seated in different parts of the room. —James Michael Newell, "The Evolution of Western Civilization," in *Art for the Millions: Essays from the 1930s by Artists and Administrators of the WPA Federal Art Project*

In rooms a third this size, L!brary artists illustrated in a varicty of mcdia—paint, pencil, taxidermy—coaxing poems, fingerprints, and life-sized portraits from students. In most cases designers converted the art into a digital medium to be vinyl-printed and applied like wallpaper, accommodating the architectural realities of unexpected building conditions revealed during construction. A lesson for students: effortlessness and grace of expression results from careful study, forethought, precision, and diligence.

Logo design by Pentagram

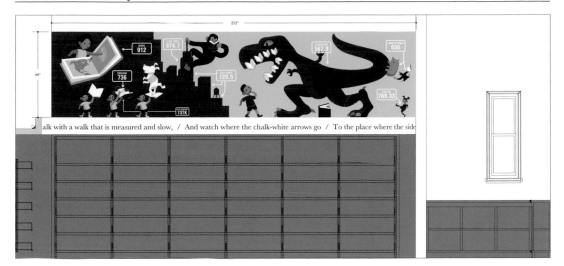

alk with a walk that is measured and slow, / And watch where the chalk-white arrows go / To the place where the side

Pentagram's two-dimensional mock-ups of murals supported the architectural documentation process, allowing construction contract bidders to estimate costs based on measured drawings and materials specifications. The design team, led by Michael Bierut, transformed works executed in a variety of media.

Elevation 4
scale: 1/2" = 1'-0"

A "garden of reading":
Digitally reassembling stock
photos, Charles Wilkin of
Automatic Art and Design
added a collage of
environments to a space
serving a high population of
students with emotional and
physical challenges at P.S.
186X.

The frieze above the
bookshelves reads:

The sun was shining on the
sea,
Shining with all his might;
He did his very best to make
The billows smooth and
bright--
And this was odd, because it
was
The middle of the night.

from "The Walrus and the
Carpenter"
by Lewis Carroll

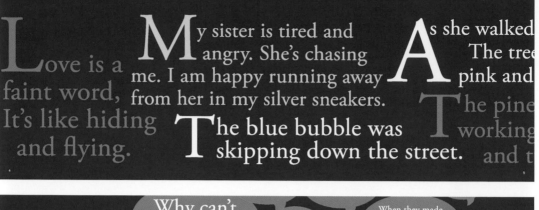

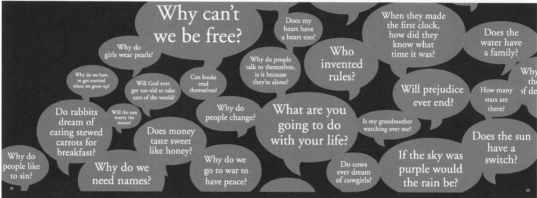

Pages are taken from a 2004 booklet created as part of the L!brary Initiative "Words for the Walls" project, titled If A Chicken Had Lips Would It Whistle?

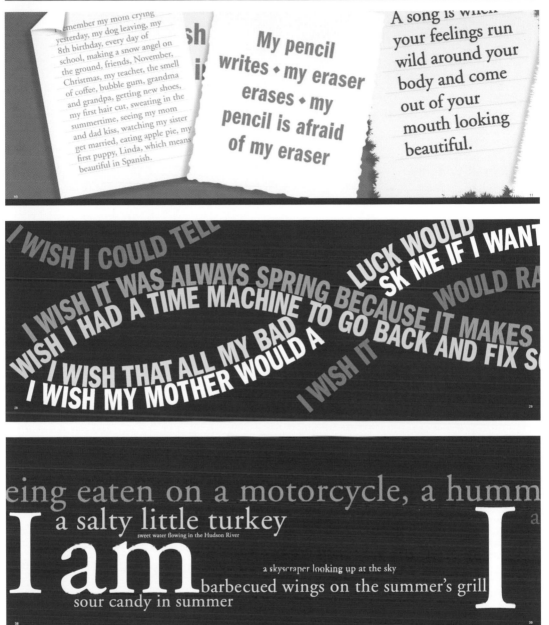

...emember my mom crying yesterday, my dog leaving, my 8th birthday, every day of school, making a snow angel on the ground, friends, November, Christmas, my teacher, the smell of coffee, bubble gum, grandma and grandpa, getting new shoes, my first hair cut, sweating in the summertime, seeing my mom and dad kiss, watching my sister get married, eating apple pie, my first puppy, Linda, which means beautiful in Spanish.

...sh i:

My pencil writes ◆ my eraser erases ◆ my pencil is afraid of my eraser

A song is w... your feelings run wild around your body and come out of your mouth looking beautiful.

I WISH I COULD TELL
I WISH IT WAS ALWAYS SPRING BECAUSE IT MAKES
WISH I HAD A TIME MACHINE TO GO BACK AND FIX S
LUCK WOULD
SK ME IF I WANT
WOULD RA
I WISH THAT ALL MY BAD
I WISH MY MOTHER WOULD A
I WISH IT

eing eaten on a motorcycle, a humm
a salty little turkey
sweet water flowing in the Hudson River
I am
a skyscraper looking up at the sky
barbecued wings on the summer's grill
sour candy in summer
I
a

Poetry and architecture by
elementary school students.
Dave Johnson, Teachers &
Writers Collaborative and
Pentagram called upon
Pablo Neruda, N. Scott
Momaday, and Willie
Perdomo to draw out
students' words.

The questions were modeled after selections from The Book of Questions *by Pablo Neruda.*

Selections from *The Book of Questions* by Pablo Neruda:

Is the sun the same as yesterday's or is that a different fire?

Is it true that in an anthill, everyone must dream?

Am I allowed to ask my book whether it's true I wrote it?

Why did the grove undress itself only to wait for the snow?

You have room for some thorns? They asked the rose bush.

Where can you find a bell that will ring in your dreams?

Does the earth sing like a cricket in the music of the heavens?

And at whom does rice smile with many white teeth?

Will Czechoslovakians or turtles be born from your ashes?

In dreams, do plants blossom and their fruit ripen?

And why does my skeleton pursue me if my soul has fallen away?

Isn't the city the great ocean of sleeping beds?

What did the tree learn from the earth, and what does it say to the sky?

Raghava KK spent ten days in the Bronx with P.S. 46X students. Every morning he met them with a canvas and they made paintings with their hands and feet, getting dirty, having fun, and mastering a visual aesthetic. Raghava's personal experience as a dyslexic child in a scholarly family taught him that the visual arts could be an important avenue for communication and a vehicle to build self-confidence.

Selected questions from Alfalfa Studio:

What is your favorite English word in the dictionary? What is your favorite word in another language?

What word most reminds you of your home?

Tell us a couple of words or a line from one of your favorite songs.

Is there a word that sounds funny to you?

Write down one or two of your favorite "slang" or "street words."

What is your favorite word from science? What is your favorite word from mathematics? What is your favorite word from sports?

What is the longest word you know?

Can you give an example of an old fashioned word? Is there one your grandmother would say?

What is a word that describes the future, or your future?

Write down a word or two you heard in the news recently.

What is a word that you always have trouble spelling?

Make up a new word of your own! Tell us what it means!

Rafael Esquer and three other artists from Alfalfa Studio led 4 teams of P.S. 196X students in a game to paint the most words in the shortest amount of time.

Original art to the left

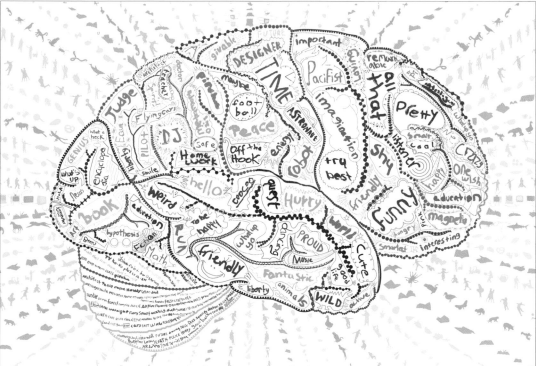

The frieze above the bookshelves at
P.S. 196X reads:
Two roads diverged in a yellow wood,
And sorry I could not travel both
And be one traveler, long I stood
And looked down one as far as I could
To where it bent in the undergrowth...

from "The Road Not Taken"
by Robert Frost

*Dorothy Kresz photographed
P.S. 10K students to float
above the room after
discovering that the school
has a high proportion of
students whose mobility is
challenged, several in
wheelchairs.*

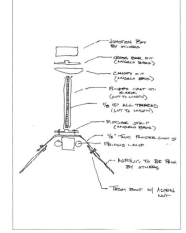

ABOVE: At P.S. 192M, two large openings bisect the room. Michael Rock of 2x4 aimed a polemical question about where education comes from, wrapping the word NATURE around the gateway to the playground outside, and the word NURTURE around the opposite threshold into the school. This is the only text in the room, save that in the books.

LEFT: An early mock-up and sketch by fabricator Veyko

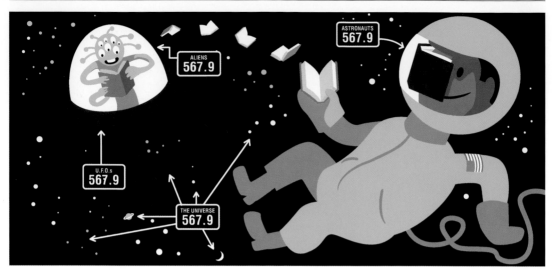

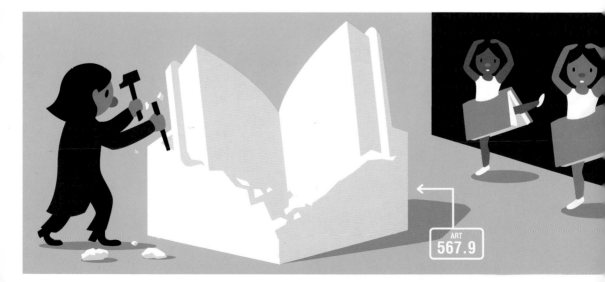

The frieze above the bookshelves at P.S. 69X reads: There is nothing like returning to a place that remains unchanged to find the ways in which you yourself have altered.

from Long Walk to Freedom by Nelson Mandela

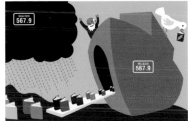

A sketch for an unused panel on "Religion" proposed by Christoph Niemann for P.S. 69X.

*Lynn Pauley used a reductive
scratchboard technique using
Carandache wax color
crayons on hot-press
illustration boards to make
portraits of students at P.S.
86X. The images were blown
up to six times original size
for print on the vinyl
wallcovering.*

Stefan Sagmeister and
illustrator Yuko Shimizu find
a truth to tell at P.S. 96X.

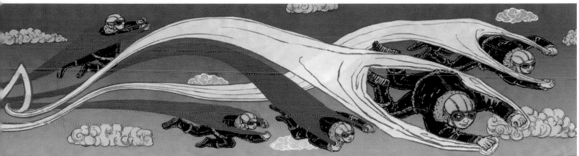

The frieze above the
bookshelves at P.S. 96X reads:
Climb every mountain
Search high and low
Follow every byway
Every path you know.

Climb every mountain
Ford every stream
Follow every rainbow
Till you find your dream.

from "Climb Every Mountain"
(The Sound of Music)
by Richard Rodgers & Oscar
Hammerstein II

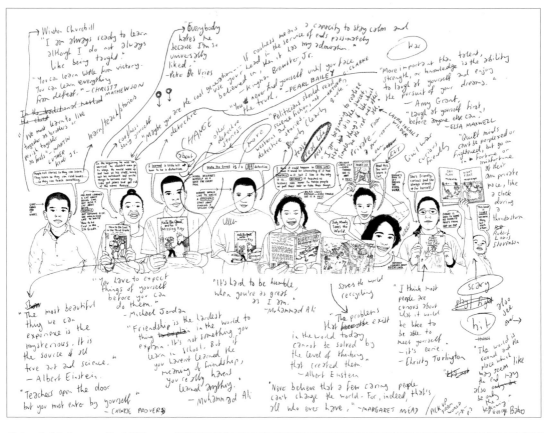

Peter Arkle transcribed P.S.
287K students' words into an
illustrated discussion of
history and literature.

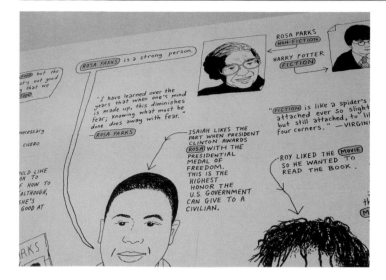

The Library
Public School 287
Brooklyn, New York

Sonata
Mallory

September 29th and 30th, 2003

Dear Boys and Girls:

Thank you for taking part in our book discussions. We are going to ask you
to think about your favorite book. We ask that you bring a copy of it with
you to the discussions. If you can't find a copy, please let Mr. Clinton know
as soon as possible. We are going to ask you to think about the following
questions before you come down to talk about your favorite book. Write as
complete an answer as you possibly can for each question.

Thank you,
Mr. Arkle, Illustrator
Mr. Clinton, Librarian

1.) What is your favorite book?

Thank you Mr. Falker

2.) Can you tell us why it is your favorite book?

well because I love
Patrica Palacco.

3.) What did you learn from this book?

I learned, not to fight
to care, and help
eachother, and care about other peoples feelings

4.) Why should people read this book?

People should read this book because
it is a really great and excellet
book

5.) What book would you write, if you were going to write a book?

I would write a book called
My daddy because he is the
best daddy ever.

LaGuabia ★

The Library
Public School 287
Brooklyn, New York

September 29th and 30th, 2003

Dear Boys and Girls:

Thank you for taking part in our book discussions. We are going to ask you
to think about your favorite book. We ask that you bring a copy of it with
you to the discussions. If you can't find a copy, please let Mr. Clinton know
as soon as possible. We are going to ask you to think about the following
questions before you come down to talk about your favorite book. Write as
complete an answer as you possibly can for each question.

Thank you,
Mr. Arkle, Illustrator
Mr. Clinton, Librarian

1.) What is your favorite book?

The cheetah girls

2.) Can you tell us why it is your favorite book?

It is my favorite book because it is
about four girls with a dream to be
professional singers but they broke up
because one of the girls were too bossy.

3.) What did you learn from this book?

If you want your dreams to come
true and you are working
together don't be bossy or they won't
want to be your friend no more.

4.) Why should people read this book?

Because if you want to be a singer
and you and your friend are doing it together
then this book might be interesting to them.

5.) What book would you write, if you were going to write a book?

I would write the cheetah girls
because it is my favorite book

RAVEN

*Maira Kalman spent a year
at flea markets shopping for
the alphabet for P.S. 47X
(fabrication and installation
by Noah Loesberg.)*

Original sketches below

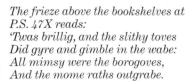

The frieze above the bookshelves at
P.S. 47X reads:
'Twas brillig, and the slithy toves
Did gyre and gimble in the wabe:
All mimsy were the borogoves,
And the mome raths outgrabe.

"Beware the Jabberwock, my son!
The jaws that bite, the claws that catch!
Beware the jubjub bird, and shun
The frumious Bandersnatch!"

from "Jabberwocky"
by Lewis Carroll

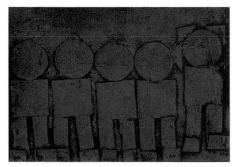

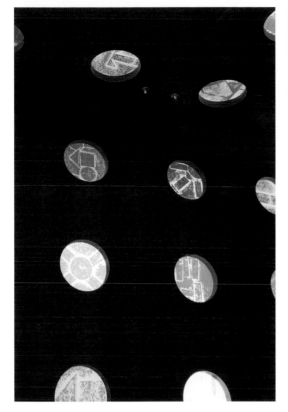

A permanent installation of back-lit punctures in a medium-density fiberboard panel marks the entry into the libraries at P.S. 31R and P.S. 110M (pictured here). Students created base drawings that were digitally printed onto Plexiglas lenses. The Hester Street Collaborative led students and teachers in workshops to generate the art, based on content in the library books. At P.S. 31R they made prints based on nature and science titles in the collection in honor of the school namesake, William T. Davis, a prominent Staten Island naturalist.

From Alphabet Workshop
Creative Writing "Toolbox"
by Dave Johnson:

MAKING METAPHOR

Eyes are windows to the soul.

A tree is a coat hangar for the sky.

A fish is a song in the eye.

The ocean is....

A violin is...

The sky is...

A wall is...

Letters are...

A clock is...

A lock is...
A necklace is...
A door is...
A dog leash is...
A drum beat is...
A baseball is...
An earring is...
A mirror is...
A street is...
A leaf is...
A map is...
A butterfly is...
A word is...
Numbers are...

The Alphabet Workshop

Hester Street Collaborative (HSC), Dave Johnson, Pentagram, four teams of architects, Robin Hood, and fifteen schools participated in workshops to promote language and design literacy and encourage personal investment in the well-being and future use of the library. Led by HSC, the group generated lesson plans and teacher training methods. HSC vetted a template for a symbol writing workshop, modifying it for each architect to accommodate unique strategies for integrating student work into the final library design.

HSC and Dave Johnson led four professional development (PD) sessions at Poet's House, a poetry library and reading room on Spring Street. Schools assigned the same architect attended in a cluster. Each school sent up to three representatives, including librarians, classroom teachers, and art educators. Afterwards, the group implemented in-school workshops with classes recommended by principals.

In the PD session, HSC and Dave Johnson modeled writing and design exercises with teachers, provided classroom materials, and facilitated a group discussion. They encouraged participating instructors to model the exercises with students before the in-school sessions in order to maximize the limited class time to solicit the children's most thoughtful results. This preparation ensured that students would be focused and teachers critically engaged in the workshops. The process provided teachers with tools and training to replicate the workshop within the future library, enlisting all the participants in the broader objective of envisioning and investing in the resource.

During the two in-school sessions, over two days, students engaged in the study and creation of writing systems through free-association exercises, translating symbols, and inventing logograms and hieroglyphs sparked by literature and poetry excerpts. Pentagram digitized the student work, converted the symbols to Illustrator line art, and scaled and reorganized it. Leroy Street Studio incorporated the work in a lighting feature. Rogers Marvel Architects decorated a casework laminate. 1100 Architect and Rockwell Group/HMA2 ornamented library walls and doors.

These symbol-language graphics are designed to encourage future generations of students to decipher their meaning and engage in the translation of the student work. The ongoing reading and interpretation of the library surfaces is another long-term goal of the final installation.
— from HSC "Participatory Workshops" report, condensed in the following pages

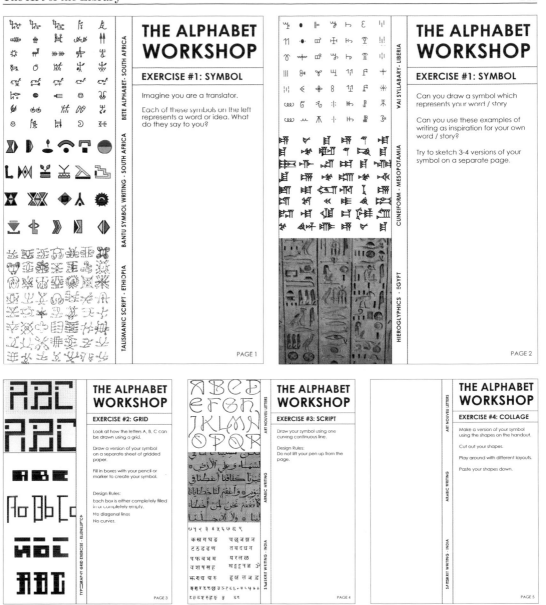

THE ALPHABET WORKSHOP

EXERCISE #1: SYMBOL

Imagine you are a translator.

Each of these symbols on the left represents a word or idea. What do they say to you?

BETE ALPHABET · SOUTH AFRICA

BANTU SYMBOL WRITING · SOUTH AFRICA

TALISMANIC SCRIPT · ETHIOPIA

PAGE 1

THE ALPHABET WORKSHOP

EXERCISE #1: SYMBOL

Can you draw a symbol which represents your word / story

Can you use these examples of writing as inspiration for your own word / story?

Try to sketch 3-4 versions of your symbol on a separate page.

VAI SYLLABARY · LIBERIA

CUNEIFORM · MESOPOTAMIA

HIEROGLYPHICS · EGYPT

PAGE 2

THE ALPHABET WORKSHOP

EXERCISE #2: GRID

Look at how the letters A, B, C can be drawn using a grid.

Draw a version of your symbol on a separate sheet of gridded paper.

Fill in boxes with your pencil or marker to create your symbol.

Design Rules:
Each box is either completely filled in or completely empty.
No diagonal lines
No curves.

TYPOGRAPHY GRID EXERCISE · ELLEN LUPTON

PAGE 3

THE ALPHABET WORKSHOP

EXERCISE #3: SCRIPT

Draw your symbol using one curving continuous line.

Design Rules:
Do not lift your pen up from the page.

ART NOUVEU LETTERS

ARABIC WRITING

SANSKRIT WRITING · INDIA

PAGE 4

THE ALPHABET WORKSHOP

EXERCISE #4: COLLAGE

Make a version of your symbol using the shapes on the handout.

Cut out your shapes.

Play around with different layouts.

Paste your shapes down.

ART NOUVEU LETTERS

ARABIC WRITING

SANSKRIT WRITING · INDIA

PAGE 5

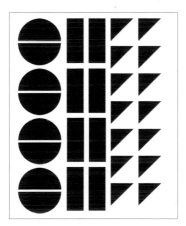

Pages from Alphabet Workshop Design workbook by Hester Street Collaborative

HSC and Dave Johnson implemented Alphabet Workshops through PD and in-school sessions in the following three variations:

With Rogers Marvel and 1100 Architect. Several short exercises with defined end products producing a diverse body of student art to accommodate fields of large-scale graphics integrated into the vertical surfaces of the library.

With Rockwell Group. Four-hour exercise emphasizing language arts literacy, encouraging students to write from excerpts from the core book collection and "translate" parts of the core collection into symbols.

With Leroy Street Studio. Exercise enhancing school's sense of ownership over the new library and building connection to the core book collection, culminating in a lighting installation designed by the architect and incorporating student art.

PD sessions
Participants: Up to three classroom instructors from each school, up to eight schools.
Part 1: Modeling (60 minutes). HSC and Dave Johnson distributed Alphabet Workshop workbooks referencing logograms throughout history from around the world. They modeled Writing and Design exercises that demystify the creative writing and graphic design processes.
Part 2: Discussion (30 minutes). Robin Hood and teachers provided feedback and discussed logistics of implementation.

In-School sessions
Participants: Fourth-grade class with a maximum of 30 students. At each school, HSC and Dave Johnson led one class with its teacher, while other teachers led additional classes.
Day 1 Prep: Prior to the in-school sessions, instructors conducted exercises from the PD workshop with participating classes.
Day 2 Prep: After Day 1, facilitators reviewed student writing and selected visually evocative excerpts not more than ten words for Day 2. Facilitators should type or print the selected excerpts onto strips of paper, and try to include selections from each student to validate creative work and encourage participation.
Materials: Workbooks, drawing media (markers, pens, pencils, paint), loose paper (plain and gridded), newsprint, easels, art postcards, dictionaries, core collection books.

The American Sign Language letters spelling READ on the wall of the P.S. 216K library expose students to silent forms of communication in a school whose namesake is the orchestra conductor Arturo Toscanini.

Exercises

Day 1: Writing (2 hours)

Discuss the new library and the students' role in the creation of artwork for its walls. Convey the importance of the task, letting them know that their work will live on in the library for years to come. Encourage students to dream big and have fun. Tailor the warm-up exercise to the energy in the room. If the students are sleepy or sluggish, start with a physical warm-up. If they are excited, start with a quiet exercise. Intersperse the workshop with stretching and breaks to maintain focus and energy.

Introduction to Writing Systems: Describe the difference between a word and symbol. Ask students to articulate the difference between reading a word and a pictogram. Spell the word "apple" slowly on the board, asking students when they can identify the word. Draw a picture of an apple on the board and ask students to describe how they know what it is. Discuss other types of symbol writing (for example, hieroglyphs). Explain to students that for the next two days we will become translators, translating images into words and words back into images.

Pictogram: a symbol that represents a word or idea
Alphabet: a system consisting of symbols that represent single sounds

Creative Writing: Dave Johnson has developed a "toolbox" of exercises that utilize translation, visual imagery, metaphor, and other linguistic devices as a springboard for creative writing. Up to four exercises can be completed in one two-hour workshop. Allow approximately ten minutes between exercises for students to exchange papers with a neighbor and read each other's work. As much as possible, depending on the size of the class and the time constraints, students should share their work, and the teaching artists should read excerpts aloud to the class. The success of this workshop depends on the facilitator choosing exercises from the "toolkit" according to the mood and attention span of the students and the size of the class.

A–Z Poem: Ask students to list three words that begin with A and continue with the rest of the alphabet to Z. At the end of the exercise, ask them to select their favorite word of the three for each letter.

Example: A - apple, angel, armor; B - birth, baggage, boy; C - cranberry, care, candle…

Free-Association Story: Ask students to create a one-page story around as many of the twenty-six selected words from the A-Z poem as possible. The goal is to quickly generate the first story that pops into their heads. Don't worry about making sense!

Denise Muniz The Day Outside
One day it was very hot. I went under an umbrella with a blanket under it. Then I went inside to get sun tan lostion out of my closet. I got my rollerblades and a bottle of water. Then my brother Daniel came out and went under the umbrella to put his rollerblades on so we can play together. It got dark and we made a fire with sticks a roasted marshmellos.

Then birds came and started eating marshmellos in the bag. Daniel made people out of stick and put it on a box. I put the blanket on the grass and looked at the moon and stars. We put out the fire. I get bread for the bird outside. Then I

Michael Gerber

MAKING METAPHOR

EYES ARE WINDOWS TO THE SOUL.

A TREE IS A COATHANGAR FOR THE SKY.

A FISH IS A SONG IN THE EYE.

THE OCEAN IS …
A VIOLIN IS…
THE SKY IS…
A WALL IS…
LETTERS ARE…
A CLOCK IS…
A LOCK IS…
A NECKLACE IS…
A DOOR IS…
A DOG LEASH IS…
A DRUM IS…
A BASEBALL IS…
AN EARRING IS…
A MIRROR IS…
A STREET IS…
A LEAF IS…
A MAP IS…
A BUTTERFLY IS…
A WORD IS…
NUMBERS ARE…

1. The ocean is a sea of moonlight

2. A butterfly is a moving rainbow.

3. A leaf is a green jacket for a tree.

4. The sky is the great sea where the sun swims.

5. A mirror is your image of what people see of you.

The GOD of morning is going to set the sun from the sky

Symbol Poems: See the pictorial writing on pages one and two of the workbook. (Examples: Bantu, Talismanic, or Chinese characters.) Ask students to translate the images. Encourage students to freely interpret, emphasizing that there is no incorrect translation. Encourage the students to free-associate and write continuously without editing. Limit the student writing to five minutes maximum. Ask students to exchange papers with a neighbor and read each other's work. Share excerpts with the class. Discuss how the logograms abstract a word/idea.

Artist's Postcards: Distribute a set of art postcards to the class, one per student, preferably prints of abstract paintings. (Examples: Marc Chagall, "I and the Village," 1911; Wassily Kandinsky, "Composition VIII," 1923.) Ask students to write a line describing their observations. After one minute, each student should pass the postcard to the left and write observations about the new card on the same sheet of paper. Shorten the allotted writing time per postcard as the exercise progresses. Continue the exercise until all the postcards have circulated around the room. Ask students to exchange papers with a neighbor and circle their favorite line from their neighbor's work and their own work.

Exquisite Corpse: This variation on Artist's Postcards combines writing from each student into one poem. Place one postcard and one sheet of loose-leaf paper on each student's desk. Each student writes a line on the paper, reacting to the imagery in the postcard at his or her station. After one minute of writing, all students fold the page down to hide the writing, and shift over one station, leaving behind the postcard and paper. The students circulate around the room, contributing a line at each station. Increase the pace as the exercise progresses. The result is a series of poems or stories collaboratively created by the entire class. For this exercise to succeed, the class must be very attentive, calm, and focused.

Writing from the Core Collection: This variation on Exquisite Corpse substitutes postcards at each station with books from the core collection. First, students practice writing a line in reaction to an excerpt the teacher has selected from a book from the core collection. After sharing some of the results of this process, students themselves select an excerpt from the book on the desk and write it on the piece of paper, followed by a blank line. After one minute of writing, each student moves to the next station, taking the piece of paper, and leaving the book. They rotate through all the stations. At the end, students fill between the lines, writing a line based on each excerpt they have chosen, like in the beginning of the exercise.

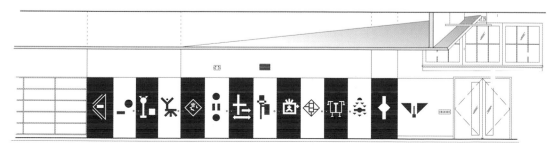

1 INTERIOR ELEVATION - SOUTH WEST
SCALE: 1/4"=1'-0"

Making Metaphor: Distribute a worksheet with a list of ideal, complete metaphors and a list of incomplete metaphors. Engage the class in a discussion of metaphor. Ask students to clarify the distinctions between a description, a simile, and a metaphor. Once the class has articulated an understanding of metaphor, ask the students to complete the unfinished metaphors on the worksheet. Exchange and share the student work.

Day 2: Design (2 hours)
Distribute an excerpt, workbook, and art materials to each student.

Symbol Writing: Use the best excerpts from Day 1 to translate poetry into a symbol. Explain that the symbol will be based on the poems, stories, and text fragments the students created, not from the words or images they selected or were given. Model the steps below and ask students to repeat with their text excerpt, in the following sequence:

Step 1: Define "symbol" as a simple, abstract representation of a word or idea. Ask students to brainstorm and consider symbols they encounter in their everyday lives. Refer to examples of abstract symbol writing in pages one and two of the workbook. Ask students to translate a symbol as a warm-up exercise.

Step 2: Underline each big idea in the excerpt.
Example: A butterfly is a rainbow in the sky

Step 3: Sketch two or three versions of each idea in the excerpt. Invite students to the board or an easel to do the same. Select one symbol per idea.

Step 4: Sketch two or three formations that combine the symbols into one compound image that represents the entire excerpt.

Step 5: Select a final version of the compound symbol. Draw it again for emphasis.

Variations:

Grid: Provide students with a grid. Ask them to translate a logogram by filling in the boxes of a grid. Each box must be entirely filled or empty.
Example: Ellen Lupton's typographic grid exercise

Script: Draw a symbol as one continuous fluid line. Try different media (marker, pencil, pen) and line weights.
Example: script typefaces, Art Nouveau typography

Collage: Using premade shapes, ask students to recreate a symbol with collaged shapes.
Example: Matisse, expressionist typography

Printmaking: Using a collaged version of a symbol, print onto colored construction paper. Hang pieces to dry.

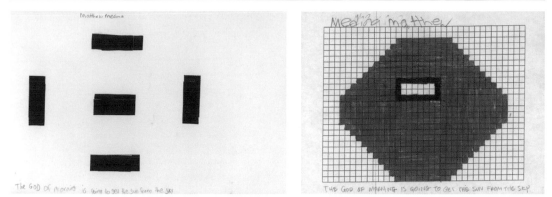

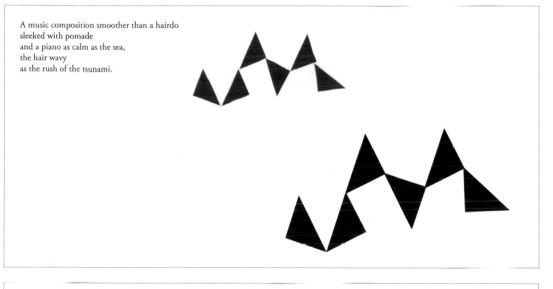

A music composition smoother than a hairdo
sleeked with pomade
and a piano as calm as the sea,
the hair wavy
as the rush of the tsunami.

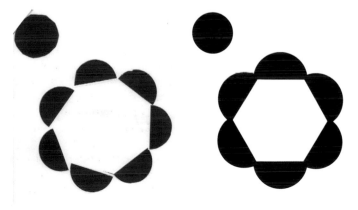

I wait for the light.
Wires climb with streets
carryinglight, carrying words,
and the birds carry messages
of the sky's imagination.

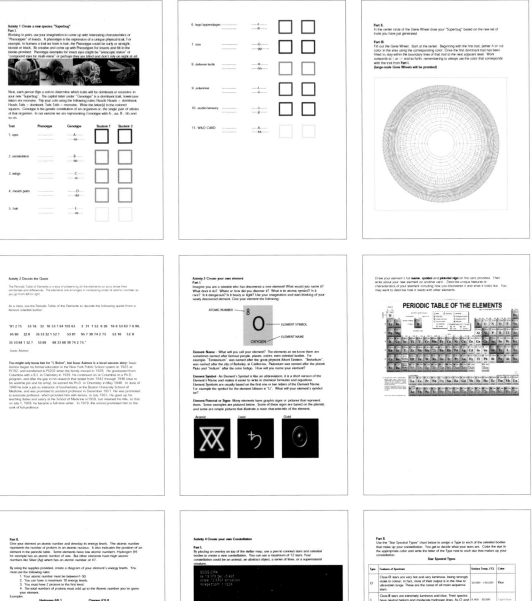

SC!ENCE

Robin Hood collaborated with Columbia University's Center for Environmental Research and Conservation, Rafael Viñoly Architects, and the educators at M.S. 88K to test the ideas behind the L!brary Initiative in a science classroom. Rafael Viñoly Architects applied its considerable experience in designing laboratories for institutions like Princeton University and the National Institutes of Health to the problem of a middle school science lab, innovating molded ergonomic seating and reconfigurable workbenches for a flexible layout to accommodate classroom-to-lab teaching styles. The architects led workshops on star spectral types, the periodic table of the elements, and genotype studies of insects. They designed the writable glass wall surface at the front of the class to be etched with patterns drawn by students onto gene wheels.

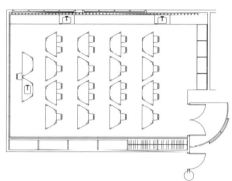

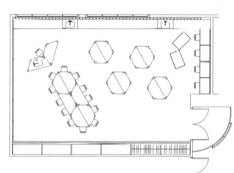

How to Make a Library

How to Make a Library

The following section culls a set of challenges and recommendations, drawing from the Robin Hood project brief and details from the various iterations of the L!brary Initiative. (So far, it has been implemented in three rounds, with varying particulars.) It relies on extensive interviews with project participants, including librarians, education experts, architects and designers, school administrators and teachers, representatives of the public agencies responsible for education and school construction in New York City, and Robin Hood staff. The design guidelines at the end of this section have been tested and reflect best practices in over fifty Initiative projects in the public schools. They were formalized after significant inquiry into library use and needs by Robin Hood and participating architects, and design review by the School Construction Authority.

Ingredients:

Creative approaches to instruction, the facilities to accommodate them, and the leadership to maximize the new resource

A funding and operations structure that distributes responsibility for library development among diverse participants

Funding that covers a period long enough for the projects to realize a strategic plan for sustainability

Architectural design that leverages the total environment to intensify learning

State-of-the-art human, technological, and literary resources

A platform to augment the library resource by enabling students' engagement with the greater community

Partnerships

The major structural challenge of an initiative like this consists of balancing and leveraging partnerships. A school system benefits most if a donation or promise of fruitful private sector partnerships is meaningful enough to warrant an overhaul of its parts. Philanthropic investment must be significant enough to underwrite major components of the project.

The public sector can validate and institutionalize an initiative. It offers a relatively stable funding stream. It can match private investments with cash or other material or human resources. A private organization can attract diverse talent. It can also act as a clearinghouse for donations, bringing together project partners who might not otherwise interact with each other. In this case, Robin Hood shouldered responsibilities as diverse as negotiating the public-private funding and operations agreement of the L!brary Initiative, providing umbrella insurance for participants in the construction venture (offsetting what would be a considerable expense for individual donors), liaising between the authorities and donors, and commissioning independent evaluations of the projects to determine areas requiring further development.

Attracting a diverse and committed network of supporters to mobilize resources was an early challenge and one of the achievements that the Initiative has been predicated upon. The spectrum of support for the funding, design and construction, equipping, maintenance, and instructional goals of the libraries is detailed in the sections below. This network has been undergirded by a good-faith partnership between the authorities involved with education and school construction in New York City (and the individual participating schools under their jurisdiction), and Robin Hood (and its network of allies providing financial support and free or reduced-cost products and services).

New York City's Department of Education has matched Robin Hood's cash investment by at least double since the inception of the Initiative. Although each party's specific responsibilities have varied with each implementation, the City has generally overseen construction (including asbestos removal—a practice that carries high liability in the private sector, the costs of which can be more easily absorbed in the public sector). The City and individual schools have shouldered the costs of educating librarians and maintaining their professional development. The City and each of the schools have been responsible for long-term maintenance of the library facilities and book collections. Robin Hood has typically provided services and products in the category of "design," hiring architects or sourcing donated services from them and their consultants, and paying for custom fixtures, furniture, and finishes that often exceeded standards for the public schools. Robin Hood has also acquired donated or reduced-cost books, technology, and the services associated with integrating these into the library.

This describes some of the macro-level funding structure, but for an initiative like this to gain momentum, partnerships must be developed at many scales and set goals that are not just cosmetic, but systemic. For example, it might be simpler for a children's book publisher to donate overstocked items to fill shelves, but more meaningful to support a qualitative institutional makeover with new titles that enhance a curriculum that serves approved high standards for education. Partnerships can form organically around areas where the initiative mission aligns with that of other institutions, like universities. Cash donors take away a personal experience and become more invested if they—and their young children—help to shelve books in new libraries they sponsored. A library ultimately becomes a revolutionary cultural driver if it stays open after school or on the weekends when parents can visit with their children.

Academic context

The most ambitious yet most fundamental ideas behind the L!brary Initiative have revolved around education. In contrast to programs that aim to incrementally reform problematic aspects of public education, this initiative undertook a bold challenge to revolutionize the library as a center for intellectual inquiry. This approach requires commitment at all educational levels.

The alchemy of the immediate intellectual environment determines whether a library like this will succeed. Overt support for the library activities by the school administration has been isolated as a critical element in the success of the resource. Principals must be willing to incorporate the library into a strategic plan to strengthen the school's instructional approach, committing funding and staff time to develop the library as a framework for impacting student performance. Teachers within a school must be willing to partner with each other to make full use of the resource. This is a radical top-down approach, but effects the greatest leverage of the initial investment.

This approach excludes schools lacking the most basic means. It requires that besides serving a high proportion of children from low-income families, schools must equally evince great receptive potential for the resource. However, this increases the equity of schools that do participate, casting them as active partners in a project.

To naturalize the resource, school leaders must build consensus at every step. Librarian training and design visioning activities can provide tangible exercises in this process. These will be addressed in the corresponding sections below.

A joint team from Robin Hood and the Department of Education reviewed applications from schools currently participating in the L!brary Initiative. Selections typically factored economic level, student performance, educational leadership, and facilities availability, using the following guideposts:

A minimum of 75 percent of students qualify to receive federal government-sponsored free or reduced-cost lunch.

A minimum of 60 percent of students read below grade level, based on English Language Arts test scores. Students show high or rising recent test scores.

Superintendents at the regional and local level endorse schools for participation, recognizing their leadership from a position outside the immediate community.

A dynamic principal and a committed teaching staff show enthusiasm for using the library to broadcast a substantial pedagogical agenda.

The school can provide 1,700 to 2,000 square feet of space in a prominent location for the library.

Schools that can budget the following for a term—the L!brary Initiative asked a minimum of five years—help the library resource to embed itself in the school and situate the school administration itself as an agent of opportunity:

> Salary lines for a full-time librarian and a technically trained paraprofessional who can relieve the librarian of operational tasks in order to focus on education.

> Book purchases to build and replenish collections. (The Initiative asked schools to match per-student funding received annually from the State of New York for books.)

> Overtime hours to staff the library on evenings, weekends, and during the summer, to encourage parents and grandparents to visit the library and read with their children—leveraging childrens' own families as the greatest motivator for scholarly curiosity and self-confidence.

Ideally, this revolutionary library forms a scaffold for broader community involvement. As an academic center, the library can gather and support excellent educational programs for children and adults sponsored by outside organizations. Many Initiative libraries host after-school literacy and tutoring programs, and Robin Hood has occasionally organized corporate volunteers to read with children in the libraries. The library can be a facility that supports ongoing philanthropic relationships. Some schools participating in the L!brary Initiative have formed relationships with publishers who regularly donate to augment their book collections. However, successful community engagement stems from the same core belief that a school initially fosters to get such an initiative off the ground: that the library should act, and be projected, as the pivotal platform for academic advancement.

Librarians

Librarians are the soul of the project. They are the very best teachers schools can access. Ideally, they are experienced actors in the school who have demonstrated dedication to the students (and perhaps even live in the neighborhood). Training them at the university level and beyond supports their work and delivers a message about the primacy of education to the school community. The expansion of their responsibilities buttresses the community and rewards deserving educators with amplified outreach and a strong opportunity for intellectual and professional development.

Educating librarians to educate children has been a cornerstone of the L!brary Initiative. Participating librarians complete a two-year graduate program, subsequent certification, and ongoing professional training. These professional credentials exceed typical requirements for elementary school librarians in New York City.

Syracuse University sponsored a specially created program of graduate coursework leading to a Master of Library Science degree, offsetting a portion of the tuition (the remainder of which is supplemented as part of the Initiative funding package). Participants enter the program as a cohort via an intensive summer session, and continue coursework online. This strategy encourages development of an informal network between school librarians. Organizing a cohort offers librarians an important professional exchange and an external reference base to help them become leaders in their own schools. This can be important in helping them to build internal school support for the library, an issue raised above.

Engaging a university to customize a program requires making the best use of its available resources and creating a model sustainable within that institution. This endeavor of the Initiative affirms the serious purpose to educate elementary school librarians. The opportunity for advancement has attracted the best teachers in each school community with a unique professional incentive. It has also demanded their commitment for at least the two-year duration of study, if not the longer expected term. The degree program has been critiqued as limiting its scope to Library Science when related coursework in Education might better help librarians serve elementary school children. Nevertheless, the program has broadened Initiative librarians' perspective. It has also offered a model of summer intensive and onsite and online training that Syracuse University has developed and extended to other New York City librarians, creating a new pipeline and pool of talent for librarian positions in the city's public schools.

Continuing education is critical. Ongoing professional training in areas from lesson planning to collection augmentation to technology literacy supplements librarians' experience. Robin Hood has sponsored offsite topic-based workshops for librarians across all the schools, and has also custom tailored onsite training in library resource development for librarians and teachers within each school. In an effort to build technological proficiency, Robin Hood has also issued laptops for academic use as part of the technology package delivered with the project.

Librarians drive the activities and perception of the library, but they do not do it alone. Besides support from the principal and other teachers within the school, as described above, a technologically trained paraprofessional to manage library operations and

collections frees the librarian from the time-consuming tasks of circulation, shelving books, and minor maintenance. This allows the librarian to devote energy to mission-specific work: enhancing methods of instruction, developing the library resource at large, and promoting the perception of the library as a significant cultural and academic center.

Design and construction
A thought-provoking library environment is a threshold. Its impact can inspire a lifelong habit of approaching the world with a curious intellect. The challenges in making such environments are familiar to practitioners of design and construction: raising capital, innovating design, and constructing libraries efficiently and cost-effectively that are durable and easy to maintain.

The L!brary Initiative mission has been compelling to professionals who offered significant assistance; Initiative architects almost uniformly raised the memory of a childhood library as a driver in their own lives. Partnerships with designers distinguish libraries aesthetically and create positive branding, fostering a favorable impression in both donors and end users. The pro bono engagement of design professionals also increases the political capital of a project as much as it reduces costs.

To facilitate and maximize the professional service donation, it is important to streamline design management and the production of documents. In the case of the L!brary

Initiative, no consistent pro bono practice was adopted. Architects, designers, and artists waived or reduced fees for at least one project, but, in many cases, also underwrote significant overhead expenses and leveraged sympathetic trade partnerships to secure in-kind contributions from engineers, fabricators, and product manufacturers.

The motivations for pro bono architectural practice often have to do with the professional satisfaction of developing a custom project for an underserved community. For the L!brary Initiative, photographers and agencies donated their professional images of the built projects to enable Robin Hood to raise thousands of dollars to support the existing libraries and promote and prolong the work of the Initiative— including its good design. Through the collective efforts of architects and the media, communities in some of the poorest neighborhoods in New York have broadcast the positive image of their schools as cultural sites. This adheres to the definition of "public good" that pro bono work is meant to address.

Nearly every Initiative library was custom designed. Many participants admire this approach for its site-specific artistic vision. It does limit the possibility of streamlining architectural production across projects, fabricating repetitive details (for instance, the bookshelf), and making scaled requests for donations to companies with the capacity to cover significant product and service costs. In the milieu of a public sector capital project, whose process transparently awards the lowest bidders meeting public qualifications, privately subsidizing custom design items supports a measure of aesthetic freedom and quality control by designers, while maintaining public accountability.

To establish transformative environments, an exceptional architectural and artistic program is as important as the concern for safe, child-friendly spaces that are easy to build and maintain. L!brary Initiative architecture has synthesized classic archetypes associated with learning, for instance, the traditional library with a focus on reading, the traditional classroom with tables and desks, and approximately eight hundred linear feet of shelving in each library showcasing books. It has also promoted alternative ideas about the architectural qualities of libraries. Bright, colorful, and architecturally stimulating rooms engage the senses through the whole environment. Soft seating—lounge chairs, throw pillows, and rugs— associates a sense of comfort with independent learning, and forms intimate places for adults to read with children. Areas where studying occurs—tables, computer workstations, easy chairs—are scaled to individuals, but have extra room for small groups to configure spontaneously, encouraging a variety of learning experiences, both private and social. The libraries often feature an area for performance. Prominent library sites within each school publicize the significance of the resource.

Involving schools in the visioning and design process offers a tangible exercise in naturalizing the library resource into the school's educational mission, building consensus around its future use, and promoting a sense of ownership about the physical facility. Soliciting students' ideas and actively involving them in generating content for architectural or graphic designs is educational and fun. Engaging teachers, principals, and custodial staff creates an important opportunity for critical feedback and significant support from the constituencies most responsible for maximizing, maintaining, and improving the resource.

Collections and equipment

Children respond with curiosity to tools that are current and culturally resonant. According to many Initiative librarians, interactive CD-ROMs, MP3 audiobooks, the Harry Potter series, and the internet are just as valuable in attracting learners as the literary canon. Also, owning pristine objects increases personal investment and self-esteem. A new book with a crisp spine is exciting to hold, and makes the reader feel equal to it. The best book collections for school libraries codify a children's literary canon, cater to specific multilingual communities, provide teaching resources, and build technological proficiencies. Outstanding libraries typically carry twenty-five volumes per student. Librarians are charged with meeting school-specific needs and maintaining currency in the collections over time.

Robin Hood typically provides Initiative libraries with a core collection of seventy-five hundred books, as well as audio and digital media. Base collections include classic and current titles, meeting standards for excellence in children's literature and the broad curricular requirements of the New York City Department of Education. Children's library experts from educational institutions like Bank Street College of Education and Columbia University, and leaders in the trade such as Follett shaped the intellectual content of the core collection, and created master lists based on academic breadth.

The installation of collections at multiple sites is a complex process. Although purchasing books or receiving donations in bulk is ideal, it requires close timing of move-in at all locations, a factor that is in part dependent upon the variables of construction schedules and school-specific issues. Current title lists change every few months as children's books go out of print, so any changes in schedule can affect orders. All books and materials must be processed for card-cataloguing, and those that are donated or retained from existing collections must undergo the time-consuming process of retrospective conversion. Optimal collections include titles from a range of publishers, so it is difficult to collect a significant quantity of donated titles from any one.

Physically putting books on the shelves is also no small matter. Besides the manual labor involved, foresight is required in developing a layout that maintains correct subject order according to the DeweyDecimal System and locates books on shelves at heights appropriate to the ages of different readers. Robin Hood has a tradition of assisting Initiative librarians in designing layout and assembling staff at the end of construction projects to help schools shelve books in their new libraries. Design requires a few hours between one staff member and a librarian marking up a floor plan, followed by some additional correspondence, and shelving is a day-long process involving ten or more volunteers. Books are typically delivered to each site in the morning, arranged on the truck in correct Dewey order for ease of shelving by a non-specialized group of volunteers.

State-of-the-art equipment and technology offer students physical mobility and media flexibility to encourage a variety of approaches to independent learning. In addition to desktop and laptop computers dedicated to the librarian and staff, libraries should have multiple desktop and laptop computers for students, and workstations with surfaces large enough to spread out to do group projects. Mobile elements—a listening station for the audio collection, a projector on a cart, a smartboard, iPods, digital cameras—allow for instruction and learning at various locations in the library, in the school at large, or outdoors, as necessary to engage with all the resources available to students in their greater environment.

Resource management, development, and evaluation

A successful library requires nurture over time. This begins with envisioning the library in the pre-construction period with the active participation of school principals, future librarians, representative teachers and students, and facilities custodians. It continues during a period in which the library is bolstered by active internal and external support from all its partners. Robin Hood and the Department of Education typically maintain close contact with the libraries during a transition period following move-in to ensure a smooth launch. Robin Hood and participating architects produced user manuals specific to public schools, tailored in content (and often graphics) to each library, including everything from as-built drawings of the custom architecture to equipment warranties and operating manuals to sample lesson plans.

After the launch, the librarian establishes pedagogy, enlists the teamwork of the teaching staff and greater community, grows the literary collection, expands the professional knowledge base, and orients students to the library resource. During this process, the project benefits from critical assessment and evaluation, most useful if

carried out by independent parties. Robin Hood sponsors independent academic evaluations of operating libraries, which have not yet produced definitive conclusions. No formal post-occupancy evaluations of facilities have been conducted yet.

The academic effect of the Initiative libraries has yet to be determined. The L!brary Initiative pilot schools have completed the five-year term stipulated for support from the major funding partners, and face the challenge of prioritizing the operation of a library in an uncertain economic atmosphere fraught with budget cuts. Their continued commitment to developing the libraries is a testament to the naturalization of these resources. Though evaluative metrics may be derived from quantifiable data such as book circulation, test scores, and other student performance criteria, the effects of these libraries might best be read in a longer-term qualitative result: the character of the future adults they produce.

Design Guidelines

The L!brary Initiative seeks to attack poverty at its roots by fostering skills and an early interest in learning that will encourage students to stay in school through high school graduation. The Initiative directs resources toward transforming spaces in schools into vibrant academic centers. The Initiative seeks to provoke imagination and inquiry-based exploration through an enhanced instructional platform, up-to-date literary collections, state-of-the-art technology, and innovative design. The new facilities communicate strong architectural and graphic messages about the power of reading and literacy.

The library is located prominently within the school.

The library is accessible to public visitors via a secure route.

The library environment is stimulating to the senses.

The library environment, furnishings, and equipment are comfortable and user-friendly for children ages 4–14, including special needs children, and to teachers, parents, and other adults.

The library is a safe, healthy, and barrier-free environment.

The library supports multiple whole class, individual, and group activities, including reading and study, project-based teaching and learning, and presentations and performances.

The library incorporates instructional signage and artifacts of student learning.

The library, its furnishings, and equipment, are durable and do not require extensive or expensive maintenance and cleaning as a result of normal use.

The library, its furnishings, and equipment adhere to sustainable design principles.

FUNCTIONAL AREAS

Entry
Clearly visible and accessible from all nearby public areas.
Bold design of doors, glazing, lighting.
Two- or three-dimensional signage including "L!BRARY" logo and plaque displaying donor names and other credits.
Views between public corridor and library.
Built-in exhibition windows to display products of library activities.
Space to accommodate several classes or small groups entering and exiting simultaneously.
Public computer with access to card catalogue: either near Entry, or part of desktop computer bank in Instructional Area.

Circulation Desk
Location for patron checkout and return of books and materials.
Control point for library, close proximity to Entry.
Primary workplace for staff, work area for 2 staff members contiguous with Circulation Desk.
Countertops: easily cleaned, maximum work surface, student height.
Perimeter to accommodate large congregations of students entering, leaving, consulting with staff.
Clear sight lines to all areas.
Proximity to a sink. Circulation Desk to provide barrier between sink and general library environment.
Storage adjacent.
Hardwired desktop computer and color printer/scanner/copier/fax.
Positioned for librarian privacy, no public or student furniture or workstations behind the Circulation Desk.
Phone with outside line for librarian to conduct research.

Presentation Area
Multimedia and multi-sensory activities, such as storytelling by librarian to younger students, student research presentations, plays.

Accommodates 30 students gathered around presenter, or in front of stage or screen.

May be demarcated by floor or ceiling finish or screen.

Soft finishes and seating.

Seating low to the ground.

Furnishing and Equipment: storyteller's chair, pull-down screen or flat surface for projection, whiteboard, 30 stackable stools or soft seating suitable for children age Pre-K and up.

Instructional Area

Learning activities for older students (grades 3 and up).

Accommodates 30 students: individual and group study and projects, teacher/librarian-led instruction, computer searches.

8 large student work tables to spread out materials.

Flexible configuration, students to work in groups of various sizes.

Space to move easily between tables and chairs in various configurations.

6 computer workstations (5, if public station is located at Entry).

1 hardwired black-and-white printer at Computer desk/tables.

Space for 2 chairs at each workstation.

Workstation to accommodate 2–3 children to spread out books and notepaper around the computer terminal comfortably.

Unobstructed view of mobile smartboard and projection screen by students at work tables.

Teaching area to accommodate teaching materials, books, notes, laptop to operate projector; access to audio-visual cart.

Unobstructed view of students by teachers and/or library staff. Ideally, students should not sit with backs to the center of room, even if this means that desks are configured so that computer screens are exposed to daylight glare.

Wireless internet access for incorporation of online resources into instruction.

Mobile audio-visual cart to hold librarian's laptop and a projector.

Mobile smartboard and audio-visual cart positioned for proper projection.

Reading Area

Small groups of students and adults, including family and community members (2 or 3 groups of 2–3 people).

Furnishings: 2 or 3 large soft chairs or small sofas, room for chairs borrowed from Presentation Area.

Not necessarily one contiguous space.

Separate from the Instructional Area; students should not have to cross the Instructional Area to access it.

Storage: Circulation Desk

Lockable storage closet or cabinets adjacent, including shelves to hold boxes of books and other materials and supplies, and a coat rack/hook.

Storage: Miscellaneous

Maximum ancillary storage space for books and supplies (this does not refer to bookshelf storage of books in collection).

Minimum 100 square feet of easily accessible, lockable storage closet or cabinets is recommended.

Supplies: miscellaneous equipment such as videos, DVDs, CDs, CD-roms, microphones, headsets, flash drives, batteries, disks, cassette or CD players, external drives, portable devices, software, manuals, cables, power strips, puppets, puzzles, games, etc.

Lockable storage and recharging capability for multiple electronic items, such as a digital camera, loose laptops, etc.

Lockable storage and recharging capability for a laptop cart.

Work table (optional).

DESIGN CRITERIA

Architectural

Open plan encouraged. Finishes, rather than partitions, are recommended to delineate Functional Areas. Visibility and clear sight lines from the Circulation Desk are critical to the smooth functioning of the library.

Hierarchy of scales and spatial variety encouraged.

Double doors required at entry, to accommodate entry and exit of two classes simultaneously.

Architectural design should reflect current ideas and practices.

Code

Design to comply with School Construction Authority and New York City code
requirements for school buildings. This includes, but is not limited to,
architectural, electrical, structural, and ventilation code requirements,
emergency power and lighting requirements, and any others that affect areas
within and around the library site.

Design to comply with American Disabilities Act requirements.

74 occupants maximum, the greatest number allowed as per current code
without causing the project to fall into the use category of Public Assembly.
Signage may be required near Entry in accordance with section 27–527 of the
New York City Building Code.

Solutions that do not require an amendment to the existing Certificate of
Occupancy are recommended. Approvals in writing may be required from the
relevant authorities.

Structural/Vibration

Structural and vibration issues should be considered, especially where removal
of load-bearing partitions necessitates structural reinforcement.

Mechanical

Temperature range: Winter 72°F–Summer 74°F.

Relative humidity range: Winter 30%–Summer 50%.

2–5 switch-operated window air-conditioning units required per room, to
accommodate continuous use of library in summer months. Existing units to be
repaired or replaced if necessary. Provide new units where none exist or
existing units are damaged beyond repair. Replace existing weathersealing
around units if damaged, or provide new where none exists.

Air-conditioning units should be placed in the top sash of the window when
possible to maintain views at eye level and maximize air circulation.

Existing radiators to remain. Although installations of fin-tube radiators
increase interior floor area up to 18 inches around the perimeter, heating
systems in older school buildings are rarely compatible with newer radiators
and coordination can become prohibitively expensive. New radiator covers
may be provided, per architect's design.

Mechanical systems and equipment replacement to be decided on a case-by-case
basis, specific to each site.

Electrical

Standard power: 110-volt.

Emergency power: required as directed by School Construction Authority or
New York City code.

Power to be provided by the School Construction Authority prior to
construction, to a 100-amp, 3-phase electrical panel within 50 feet of the library
site, or to a panel that meets minimum power requirements per architects' and
engineers' design.

Minimum distribution of receptacles: 2 duplex receptacles per 8 linear feet or 2
pairs of duplex receptacles per 20-foot wall. Additional duplex receptacles at
Presentation Area and Instructional Area. Many of the items to be plugged in
have power packs that cover the entire receptacle.

Provide several duplex receptacles at Storage: Miscellaneous for recharging
miscellaneous electronic equipment.

Dedicated receptacle at each air conditioner, with appropriate power.

Dedicated receptacle at designated laptop cart plug-in point, with appropriate
power.

Lighting

Maximize daylighting.

ES standard lighting levels: 15–30 footcandles.

Design lighting levels (standard): 15–30 footcandles.

Design lighting levels (reading level): 40–50 footcandles.

Fluorescent lighting required. Incandescent lighting discouraged.

Easy and cost-efficient bulb replacement at fixtures required. Consult with
school custodian prior to design.

Project documents should specify 10 percent overstock of each lamp type.

Minimize lamp types. Match the schools' existing lamp types. Unique fixture
design is preferred over unique lamp types.

Communications

Telephone required. Phones should ideally support intra-school use and one
outside line. Librarian phone time is often spent with vendors, parent
volunteers, and others outside school. Provide duplex receptacle at Circulation
Desk for phone and fax.

Fax machine required at Circulation Desk. Provide duplex receptacle at
Circulation Desk for phone and fax.

Fiber and category-5 data cabling outside library site to be provided by School
Construction Authority prior to construction, to a designated switch location.

New public announcement or intercom system not included in scope of work.

Existing public announcement or intercom system to remain. Relocation or
replacement of devices acceptable, per architect's design and School
Construction Authority approval, but discouraged except in cases where
devices are located on a partition to be removed.

Plumbing

New plumbing not included in scope of work.

Plumbing for only 1 sink to remain where 1 or more sinks exist at site. New
fixture and casework may be provided, per architect's design. Proximity to
Circulation Desk recommended. Sinks are useful because of the librarian's
frequent exposure to dust in handling books and in special needs classes where
additional staff may be required to escort students to the bathroom.

All sinks to be capped off prior to construction.

W.C. maintenance or replacement to be decided on a case-by-case basis, specific
to each site.

Fire Protection

Existing fire alarm and smoke detector system to remain. Relocation or
replacement of devices acceptable, per architect's design, New York City code
compliance, New York City Fire Marshal inspection, and School Construction
Authority approval, but discouraged except in cases where devices are located
on a partition to be removed or modification is required per code.

Existing sprinkler system to remain in cases where system exists except in
cases where system interferes with a partition to be removed (as permitted by
code) or modification is required per code.

Fire alarm and sprinkler systems to comply with New York City Building Code
requirements for fire protection in school buildings. Work outside library site
to be provided by School Construction Authority prior to construction, to
connection points within site to be determined by architect.

Partitions, doors, and glazing separating library and public corridor to comply
with New York City building code requirements for fire-rated separation in
school buildings.

One fire extinguisher (minimum) required as per New York City Fire
Department requirements.

Health/Safety

All asbestos-containing materials to be abated and other hazardous materials to
be removed from site prior to construction. Site assessment and abatement/
removal of hazardous materials to be performed by School Construction
Authority.

Low-VOC materials should be specified wherever possible to reduce off-gassing.

Libraries may open to public and students immediately after construction.

All surfaces to be durable, smooth and free of splinters and cracks.

Rounded corners recommended at all millwork and
furniture.

At bookshelves, reinforcement required to prevent shelf imbalance if pressure
applied to front edge.

Mobile tables must have lockable casters. Tables must be supported on corners,
not on pedestals.

All finishes to be certified hypoallergenic. Carpeting is discouraged due to the
high incidence of asthma among New York City schoolchildren.

Floor surfaces to be soft, durable, non-slip, and easy to clean/maintain.

4 sets of keys to be provided for all locking doors. Keying to be coordinated with
building keying.

Self-closing, lockable double doors required at Entry.

All storage closets and cabinets to be lockable. Self-closing doors not required at
closets.

All radiators to be covered. Removable covers required for access to valves and
pipes.

Internal wire management required at all workstations, particularly at the
Circulation Desk, public computer, student computer workstations.

Circulation Desk computer to be shielded by removable protective panel barring
student access to plug and cable points at back of computer. Computer is often
positioned with its back to students and visitors.

Wire glass is discouraged for use below door header height due to the exposure
of sharp wire if glass is shattered.

No power or data drops in floor in heavily trafficked areas. Where floor drops are unavoidable, they should be shielded from dirt, grime, and student access.

Security
New security system not included in scope of work.
Existing security system to remain. Relocation or replacement of devices acceptable, per architect's design and School Construction Authority approval.

Millwork
(items below may be designed as built-in millwork or freestanding furniture)
Millwork design to accommodate weight and configuration of items supported, including but not limited to books, equipment, computers, etc. Design to incorporate apron stiffeners, cross-bracing, and other vertical and lateral reinforcement as necessary.

Bookshelf
Design and location to facilitate browsing and easy replacement of books.
Slip-resistant finish required.
2–14 books per linear foot required, minimum.
Collection size:
  10,000-volume collection, minimum. Accommodation should be made for collection to grow beyond a 10,000 volume collection. Outstanding libraries typically have 25 books per student. Linear feet of shelving should be maximized, but 800 linear feet is approximately the minimum required.
  2,000 volumes at Presentation Area, with picture books and titles for younger readers. Approximately 150 linear feet of shelving, minimum.
  4,000 non-fiction volumes (approximately 300 linear feet of shelving, minimum) and 1,000 reference volumes (approximately 75 linear feet of shelving, minimum) at Instructional Area.
  3,000 fiction volumes (approximately 225 linear feet of shelving, minimum) at Reading Area.
Shelving units:
  Perimeter shelving units to contain no more than 5 shelves, at 74 inches above the finished floor, maximum. Shelves above this height for display purposes only, and must not house any portion of 10,000-volume requirement for collection. Top shelf containing books must be no higher than 60 inches above the finished floor.
  Interior shelving units to contain no more than 3 shelves, at 46 inches above the finished floor, maximum. Top shelf containing books must be no higher than 42 inches above the finished floor. Exceptions will be considered on a case-by-case basis, provided they do not create impediments to sightlines across the facility.
  Low shelving required at Presentation Area for oversized or picture books. Higher shelving acceptable at Instructional Area. Younger students should not have to reach a high shelf to acquire picture books or other appropriate titles. Older students should not have to disturb a younger class in the Presentation Area to acquire a book for older readers. The top two shelves of high shelving cannot be reached by many students.
  Signage describing the collection to be provided within a unit at one location per unit. Signage describing specific collection range to be provided at each shelf.
  Vertical shelf supports to be 36 inches on center, maximum. All vertical supports to align above and below, to facilitate Dewey Decimal Cataloging.
  Bracing required in gypsum wallboard partitions where shelves supported by partition.
  Adjustable shelving to accommodate shifting book collection. If horizontal datum lines are desired for visual regularity, consider setting the top and bottom shelves proud, and recessing the middle shelves. Very few areas of the collection have books of a standard height.
  Bottom shelf 4 inches above the finished floor, minimum.
Shelves:
  Dimensions: 12 inches deep, ¾-inch thick maximum. 13 inches minimum clear height between shelves. At fiction section, 10 inches minimum clear height between shelves is possible, but adjustable shelving is preferred, as the location of portions of the collection tends to shift over the years. At oversize picture books section, 20–30 inches clear height is recommended.
  Label holders at horizontal edge.

Circulation Desk
Dimensions: 36 inches deep, minimum, ample knee space required, maximize length to accommodate 1 librarian + 1 staff paraprofessional to use desk simultaneously, with computers and equipment as required.

Easily cleanable work surface for librarian and/or library staff; for processing
  new books, preparing instructional material, and other routine activities.
Mobile or built-in lockable cabinet under desk.
Storage for 2 mobile book carts under or behind desk.
Lockable book return/drop location. This may be built-in millwork, or a safe/
  lockbox.

Computer desk/table(s) at Instructional Area
Dimensions: 36 inches deep, minimum, ample knee space required. Maximize
  length to accommodate computers and equipment as required.
Desk/table length to accommodate seating around 6 workstations (or 5, if 1
  workstation is located at Entry). Space required for 2–3 students to cluster
  around each computer and spread out books and papers.

Computer desk/table at public station at Entry (Optional)
Dimensions: 36 inches deep, minimum, ample knee space required. Maximize
  length to accommodate computer and equipment as required. Desk length to
  accommodate seating around workstation, if not located at Computer desk/
  table.

Storage shelving at closets/cabinets
Dimensions: 12 inches deep, minimum, 72 inches top shelf height, maximum, to
  accommodate books, supplies, miscellaneous devices.

Finishes
Finishes to be soft, bright, colorful, durable, easily maintained and cleanable.
Laminate flooring must be stringently warrantied for product and installation.
  Floor tile preferred; seamless vinyl requires extra care by custodial staff, is
  difficult to replace when damaged.
No wall-to-wall carpet or carpet tiles. Area rugs recommended.
Ceilings to facilitate maintenance and cleaning. Dropped ceilings discouraged.
Flat latex paint at ceilings, eggshell finish required at walls, semi-gloss finish
  required at locations where vinyl wallcovering to be applied.
  Vinyl wallcovering adheres only to semi-gloss paint finish.
10% overstock of finishes, such as flooring tiles, should be provided in
  specifications.

Graphic Design
2-D or 3-D L!BRARY logo by Pentagram to be located at Entry.
Graphics at window shades ok.
Graphics to be integrated with architectural design concept.
Graphic design should celebrate learning, literacy, the school population, and
  particularly the students. Graphics should be as universal as possible and
  speak to future generations of students as well as to current student
  population. Graphic design should reflect current ideas and practices.
Communication and collaborative work with students and teachers at school is
  recommended to generate artwork and graphic content. The library is
  intended to promote literacy on various levels (including design literacy) and to
  encourage the school's sense of ownership of the library.

Display
Delineated portions of vertical surfaces in Instructional Area to be tackable, for
  display of student work and instructional material. No fabric finishes.
Tackable surfaces to accommodate staples. Thumbtacks/pushpins not allowed in
  schools.
Shelving tops at all heights, radiator enclosure tops, and other horizontal
  surfaces to facilitate display of books, student work, and other materials.
Display cases for the hallway outside the library to be provided where possible.
  Where design calls for removal of display cases, they should be carefully
  salvaged and returned to school

Furniture
Furniture to be soft, bright, colorful, durable, easily maintained and cleanable.
Furniture to be easily used and easily stored/stackable.
Circulation Desk:
    2 ergonomic work chairs on casters.
Presentation Area:
    32 stools (seat height approximately 16 inches above the finished floor) or
      soft seating/cushions for students. Must be stackable.
    1 comfortable chair for storytelling.
    Shelving or storage for oversized books may be designed as built-in
      millwork or freestanding furniture.

Instructional Area:

> 32 chairs (seat height 16–17 inches) for students and adults, proportioned to table surface heights. Must not be on casters.
>
> 8 tables (surface height 26–27 inches, 42–48 inches in diameter or width) to seat 4 students each, with room to spread out books, papers, and laptops. Tables must be able to be clustered.
>
> Computer desk/table(s) may be designed as built-in millwork or freestanding furniture.
>
> Space for 2 chairs for each workstation (seat height 16–17 inches) at computer desk/table(s) and optional public station. Seats for students and adults, proportioned to desk/table surface heights. Bench seating ok, but not recommended.

Reading Area:

> Soft seating, for 4–6 students or adults. Minimum 25% of seating to accommodate elderly visitors.

Storage: Circulation Desk:

> Shelving may be designed as built-in millwork or freestanding furniture.

Storage: Miscellaneous:

> Shelving may be designed as built-in millwork or freestanding furniture.

Fixtures

Intentionally left blank.

Equipment

Lock-down hardware required at all computer-related and audio-visual equipment.

2 large mobile carts for books.

1 whiteboard in Presentation Area.

Circulation Desk: All equipment to be kept out of reach of students.

2 spinners, 5 shelves high, arms deep enough to hold paperback books and magazines. Lockable spinner arms preferred. Rotating base with pockets preferred, to hold magazines. Must be stable.

Technology

Lock-down equipment required as indicated below.

Operating system software to be specified for desktop and laptop, per Department of Education standards.

All monitors to be flat-screen.

Computer screens should not face windows to avoid glare, unless windows are north-facing.

Circulation Desk: Barcode reader and computer, located appropriately to accommodate book check-out.

Hardware

5 desktop computers (with monitor, CPU, keyboard above or below desktop, mouse, speakers and earphones, and lock-down device) at computer desk at Instructional Area.

1 desktop computer (with barcode reader, monitor, CPU, keyboard above or below desktop, mouse, speakers and earphones, and lock-down device) at Circulation Desk.

1 public computer (with monitor, CPU, keyboard above or below desktop, mouse, speakers and earphones, and lock-down device) either at Entry, visible from the Circulation Desk so that the librarian may assist a lone user if necessary, or in line with 5 desktop computers at Computer desk/table(s) in Instructional Area so that it may be used by a class. This computer should not be located at the Circulation Desk.

5 student laptops with wireless cards installed, and earphones, on laptop cart.

1 librarian laptop with wireless card installed, and earphones, on laptop cart.

1 mobile chargeable lockable laptop cart at Instructional Area or Storage: Miscellaneous. Dimensions: 24 inches wide by 18 inches deep by 26–42 inches high.

1 color printer/scanner/copier/fax machine at Circulation Desk and one black-and-white printer at Computer desk/table(s) in Instructional Area, both hardwired and with lock-down hardware.

Barcode reader at Circulation Desk.

Server for the card catalog system if the server is not located offsite.

Cabling and Wiring

Preparatory infrastructural work outside library site to be performed by School Construction Authority prior to construction. Power must be pulled from the School's main wiring closet to a 100-amp, 3-phase electrical panel within 50 feet of the site. Fiber and category-5 duplex data network cabling to be run from School's data closet to a switch within the library. No patch panel required.

Hardwiring required at all computer workstations, printers, wireless access points, and designated points at Presentation Area and Instructional Area. Computers and printers to receive duplex data wiring; wireless access points typically require one wire.

Line voltage to be rigid conduit or EMT Electricity. New York City code compliance required for wiring.

Isolated ground bus receptacles or other adequate surge protection to be provided for all computer and computer-related equipment.

Wireless access points to be mounted approximately 96 inches above finished floor at opposite ends of library. Access points to be elevated for performance reasons and hardwired. (Alternate: data and power receptacles within 3 feet.) Access points must not be placed under fluorescent light (optional power and data receptacles to be located appropriately). Devices must not be attached to a shelf.

Voice/data: Category-5 (unshielded twisted pair cable) data wiring to all desktop computers, printers, and wireless devices. Approximately 3 wireless devices per library site.

Telephone and fax receptacles required adjacent to or within Circulation Desk. One phone line, 2 jacks required (one jack each for phone and fax machine).

Phone: Category 5e unshielded twisted pair cable for voice (4 pair twisted, #24 AWG).

Data and power can be run through:
    ¾-inch floor conduit
    gypsum wallboard partitions
    dropped ceiling (and vertical runs from ceiling)

Software

Operating systems at all desktops and laptops.

Card catalog system to be accessible online. Site license to be purchased for access from all computers.

Word programming software at all desktops and laptops.

Graphics software at all desktops and laptops.

Audio-Visual

Lock-down equipment required for all technology housed in public areas of library.

1 LCD video/data projector.

1 lockable mobile cart for audio-visual equipment.

1 mobile smartboard for Instructional Area.

1 mounted pull-down projection screen for Presentation Area.

(optional) 1 mounted pull-down projection screen in Instructional Area

1 television.

1 video/DVD player (possibly combined with television).

1 lockable mobile cart for television and video/DVD player.

1 stereo system with tuner, amplifier, tape and CD player, and speakers. Dual cassette capability preferred.

Listening station for 4–6 students to use simultaneously. Earphones should have individual volume controls, possibly through connection with the stereo. Jackbox must be compatible with any audio source, including microphone.

1 lockable mobile cart for stereo and listening station.

1 microphone.

1 MP3 player.

1 digital camera.

Acoustics

Noise criterion level: NC–30.

Sound transmission coefficient: STC–55.

Miscellaneous

Department of Education will be responsible for maintenance and upkeep of library facilities after construction, following design specifications by architect.

Window treatments to be easy to operate, minimize/eliminate glare, and darken room when deployed.

Coat rack/hook required at Storage: Circulation Desk.

Plaque displaying donor names required at Entry.

Project Manual required at project closeout.

The following information should be included in the Project Manual, on the title drawing sheet and on other appropriate drawing sheets:
    PS/MS number(s) & school name
    School address & phone number

School region number
Principal name & contact number(s)
Head of custodial services name & contact number(s)
Assistant principal name & contact number(s)
Librarian name (librarians to be selected) & contact numbers
Gross and net area of library (also on construction plan and furniture plan)
Linear feet of shelving (also on construction plan and furniture plan)
Book count (also on construction plan and furniture plan)
Key plan showing location of library within footprint of floor (in title block on
  all sheets)
Floor number that library is located (in title block on all sheets)

APPENDIX

L!BRARY logo (by Pentagram).
Specification for plaque displaying donor names (by Pentagram).
Technology standards for hardware and software (by Custom Computer).

Index

Note: Italicized page numbers indicate
illustrations.

Photo Credits

1100 Architect
94, 95(tl, tr)

Alfalfa Studio
116(middle 2)

Peter Arkle
133(t)

Kevin Chu/KCJP
11, 13, 60, 61(b), 67(l, br), 125(bl, br), 176

Dean/Wolf Architects
21(ml, mr, b)

Gluckman Mayner Architects
121(b)

Jeff Goldberg/Esto
77, 78, 87(t, m), 89

Hester Street Collaborative
138, 145

Marpillero Pollak Architects
51(bl, middle 6: tm, bl)

Paul Warchol Photography
84, 85, 86, 89(m)

Peter Mauss/Esto
4-5, 17, 19(m), 20, 21(t), 23(bl), 33, 37, 38-39, 40, 43, 46-47, 51(t, br), 52, 53(t), 55(tl, tr), 56(l), 57, 64–65, 66, 67(tr), 68(l, r), 69, 72, 73(l), 75, 93(t), 95(b), 96–97, 99, 100, 112, 113(t), 114, 120, 121(t), 123(t), 124, 125(t), 130, 133(b), 134, 135, 136, 137, 139, 143, 147(tl, bl)

Katie Murray
87(b)

Henry Myerberg
55(bl)

Jock Pottle/Esto
89(top 4)

Richard Lewis Architect
106, 107, 116(t, b), 117, 128

Robin Hood
18, 24, 36, 41, 42(r), 44(br), 51 (middle 6: tl, tr, bm, br), 53(b), 54, 55(br), 56(r), 73(b), 74, 93(b), 113(b), 115, 131

Rogers Marvel Architects
147(tr, br)

Tod Williams Billie Tsien Architects
42(l), 44(t, bl)

Albert Vecerka/Esto
61(t), 62, 63, 80, 81

Ken Wyner
22

Back cover:
Peter Mauss/Esto, P.S. 47X*(tl)*
Peter Mauss/Esto, P.S. 32X*(tm)*
Peter Mauss/Esto, P.S. 184K*(tr)*
Jeff Goldberg/Esto, P.S. 42Q*(bl)*
Peter Mauss/Esto, P.S. 192M*(bm)*
Peter Mauss/Esto, P.S. 69X*(br)*

Acknowledgments

Many sponsors made it possible to chronicle this remarkable project.

Public Architecture encouraged the book from its inception and secured necessary institutional sponsorship. The National Endowment for the Arts generously underwrote the manuscript. The American Institute of Architects supported preliminary research. Each architect, artist, photographer, and agency, as credited, donated the imagery within. Pentagram designed the book, helped to seek a publisher, and assisted at every step. Princeton Architectural Press made this publication a reality. Robin Hood provided the spirit behind the project and hours of proofreading, and granted me a unique perspective of humanitarian work.

I wish to thank all the individuals whose acknowledgement has been limited to their affiliated institutions, organizations, or firms, and any L!brary Initiative participants who may have been overlooked due to the breadth of this project. Each person named within these pages, and many whose names do not appear, shared important insights that I have tried to capture accurately. Several individuals gave interviews, read drafts, and helped in myriad other ways.

Robin Hood provided critical support for this publication. David Saltzman's encouragement and perspective have been invaluable. Michael Weinstein, Laurie Fabiano, and Mark Bezos were crucial angels. The manuscript owes a debt to Emary Aronson, Mali Locke, Scott Lauer, and Jennifer Pitts who shared insights from work on the Initiative. Megan Wyatt has been an indispensable resource. Lonni Tanner kindly shared her experiences and ebullient vision for an initiative that she brought into being.

Scores of principals and librarians in the five boroughs, too many to list here, gave up precious time to show me around and be interviewed. Former Chancellor Harold Levy's generosity and the imagination of his once Executive Assistant Jonathan Levi brought new dimensions to my understanding of the L!brary Initiative; they reinforced the manuscript with the inspired thinking they put behind the libraries. Stephanie Dua contributed a unique viewpoint as the current CEO of the Fund for Public Schools and former Robin Hood staff member. I also thank her helpful team, including Mary Schacherbauer, Lara Holliday, and Arlene Dominguez. Barbara Stripling at the NYC Department of Education, Bank Street librarian Lisa Von Drasek, and Eden Ross Lipson taught me about children's libraries.

Space does not permit me to individually thank each architect, designer, and artist, and their team members, for their inspiring pro bono spirit, their obvious genius, and the personal encouragement each of them gave me. Michael Bierut at Pentagram imagined this book long ago and infused its pages with the same enthusiasm he showed for the built projects. His assistant Tamara McKenna has been a rock. I thank each photographer for the significant gift of images that make this book what it is. Erica Stoller's personal interest has been an inspiration and source of moral support. Wendy Hurlock Baker at the Smithsonian Archives of American Art and Catherine Townsend with Capitol Hill Community Foundation's School Libraries Project each located necessary images in the nick of time. For early advice on publication, I thank Chuck Kim at the Cooper-Hewitt, and Neal Johnston, Esq. For promotion I thank Miyuki Arikawa at the Aspen Institute and Kirsten Lodal at LIFT.

Many thanks to Jennifer Thompson, Lauren Nelson-Packard, Dan Simon, and Bree Apperley at Princeton Architectural Press, and to Kevin Lippert for backing this project at a critical moment. For interrupting busy schedules to thoughtfully critique drafts, I thank Adi Shamir at the Van Alen Institute, Bryan Bell at Design Corps, John Peterson at Public Architecture, Rosemary Wakeman at Fordham University, Caren Rabbino at Fast Forward Consulting, Igor Siddiqui at University of Texas at Austin, Gretchen Schneider at Schneider Studio, Trina Deines at University of Washington, and Michael Waters at New York University. Jean-Louis Cohen at the Institute of Fine Arts at New York University has been a tremendous support and influence on my understanding of politics, history, and architecture. Finally, this book simply would not exist if not for the indefatigable John Cary at Public Architecture.

A few cheerleaders have logged hours of buttressing, promoting, and childcare. Thanks to Azania Andrews, Kieran McGrath, Julie Werry, Jason Gold, Anne Frederick, Hester Street Collaborative, Katy Brennan, Quang Bao, Rayaan Shums, Sanjive Vaidya, Elzbieta Kosakowska, the Hassebroek, Passi, Robb, and 214 Riverside families, Shoma Lahiry, and Kerstin Park-Labella.

Family makes everything possible. Many things have been possible for me because of my mother, who took me to my first library, my father, who read to me at night, and a little brother who let me teach him the alphabet. For my husband's parents, learning is as natural as affection. His entire family is an inspiration as I try to raise a son to value education.

My heartfelt thanks for the whole family, and especially for Dr. K. Venkata Raman, Shanta Raman, Dr. Hafiz G.A. Siddiqi, Najma Siddiqi, Sarat Raman, Suzanna Egolf, Dina Siddiqi, David Ludden, Mohona Siddiqi, and Sonia Raman.

For Asif and Sahil, my joys and sighs.